ENGAGED CITIZENS, INSPIRED THINKERS, READY FOR A NEW TOMORROW

OUR SHARED STORY

COPYRIGHT © 2010

HAPPY VALLEY MIDDLE SCHOOL

ALL RIGHTS RESERVED

ISBN 978-0-557-40974-7

HAPPY VALLEY MIDDLE SCHOOL
13865 SE KING ROAD, #B
HAPPY VALLEY, OREGON 97086
503.353.1920
HTTP://WWW.NCLACK.K12.OR.US/HVALLEYMID

DEDICATION

To the students, staff, and community of Happy Valley Middle School.

CONTENTS

Principal's Forward..........................vii - ix

Acknowledgements............................x - xi

Introduction............................*Page 1*

Acceptance...........................*Pages 3 - 70*

Courage..............................*Pages 71 - 90*

Empathy..............................*Pages 91 - 110*

Friendship...........................*Pages 111 - 124*

Hope.................................*Pages 125 - 168*

Integrity............................*Pages 169 - 192*

Interdependence......................*Pages 193 - 206*

Laughter.............................*Pages 207 - 220*

Love & Kindness......................*Pages 221 - 242*

Perseverance.........................*Pages 243 - 270*

Pride................................*Pages 271 - 282*

Various Themes.......................*Pages 283 - 307*

Principal's Forward

The novelist and poet, Ursula Le Guin wrote, "The story - from *Rumpelstiltskin* to *War and Peace* - is one of the basic tools invented by the human mind, for the purpose of gaining understanding. There have been great societies that did not use the wheel," she wrote, "but there have been no societies that did not tell stories."

I believe in the power of story. In college, I was an English and Religion double major, spending days and nights reading from various anthologies and interpreting the philosophies and the histories from many of the world's great religions. But looking back at my time at Saint Olaf College, it is clear that my path to these majors was not deliberate or even planned. It was the result of a continued exploration of classes and experiences that were grounded in the common themes found in the stories of our lives.

During my first two years at Saint Olaf, you could say I was rather fickle. I wandered in and out of majors, first declaring history, then psychology and philosophy. I took strange course loads with incongruent classes like Renaissance Art History with Stellar and Galactic Physics. My friends, on the other hand, were laser-like in their focus. Somehow they knew from their very first classes that they were biology majors, economics and math majors. I was always rather envious of their focus. It wasn't until my junior year that my advisor pointed out the seemingly obvious. While dabbling with courses from various other disciplines, I had gathered enough credits to put me on track for a double major.

Though my senior year was frantic, it proved to be a turning point in my life. By exploring various courses and ideas, I finally came to the realization that many others had reached before me; that no matter the content, issue or conflict, story is the glue that binds our society. I am not sure why it had taken me sixteen years of formal schooling to reach this realization, but there it was, waiting for me to explore further in my senior research project.

Looking back at the experiences of my life, I cannot recall with clarity all the stories I have read and learned or even all the people I have met or at one time called friends. The vitality of many of the characters from my life has been lost to faded memories, to places blurred and sometimes forgotten. Yet, I know, while I cannot recall each of the stories that have enriched my life, they have. They are like the many names of the hundreds of students that come in and out of our schools each year. While names will eventually fade over time, the collective story will remain, helping us all to write and rewrite the work of our lives.

I believe that story is the greatest gift we have to offer and to receive.

This year, we successfully traversed the challenges of opening a new school. And to date, we have written our prologue. In newness and esthetic beauty, we are truly blessed. However, the physical structure of our school is just the setting of our shared story. As a new school, the collective stories of our student body, staff, and community represent the parts that will ultimately define us.

This book contains snapshots of our shared stories. In the tradition of *This I Believe®*, an international project that engages people in composing and sharing essays describing the core values that guide their lives, we have begun to write and archive our stories. Our stories are rooted in the common concepts that we believe unite us as a school community: **Acceptance, Empathy, Hope, Interdependence, Integrity,** and **Pride**. With a deeper understanding of these core values, and by sharing our stories, our school can continue to grow together, celebrate writing and storytelling, and form a lasting tradition.

-Christopher Boyd
April 2010

Acknowledgements

Thank you students and staff for sharing part of your story, embracing our differences, and celebrating the similarities that unite us. Through your many voices, we have created a school community that will enrich and empower the lives of students for many years to come.

Happy Valley Middle School Staff

Nick Adams
Michelle Arko
Laurence Baldwin
Jeff Betts
Christopher Boyd
Karen Chadwick
Kelly Dwight
Jill Ellison
Jared Englund
Jessica Goff
Julie Harris
Fred Harvey
Tom Higginbotham
Leanne Hogan

Sara Idle
Lisa Jacobson
Rose Janusz
Denise Jeseritz
Sandi Johnson
Kim Johnston
Gladys Kandel
Dianne Kirkpatrick
Nadia Kushniyuk
Tracey Lankton
Emily Leeson
David Liebenstein
Jim Lippert
Erika Lockwood

Connie Lorimor
Shelley Lute
Abigail McAuley
Karen McCord
Marti McLain
Gayle Matthews
Arman Mirani
Sue Moore
Shirley Naso
Megan Neal
Ecaterina Nedelco
Steve Oliver
Mike O'Malley
Nancy O'Shea
Ashley Press
Maureen Ray

Hilary Richardson
Linda Rua
Becky Schumacher
Karen Schweitzer
Debbie Skiles
Meagan Sternberg
Kathleen Strobel
Linda Tinkham
Jan Tommaso
Georgia Uhlar
Julie Walker
Bill Welch
Valerie Whitehead
Naomi Whitmarsh
Nancy Wiebelhaus
Megan Willis

INTRODUCTION

Happy Valley Middle School opened its doors for the first time in September 2009. It is one of four middle schools in the North Clackamas School District, serving over 630 students, grades seven and eight.

As a new school, the staff is committed to developing life-long learners and proficient writers. As part of this commitment, Happy Valley Middle School engaged in a building-wide writing project entitled, *This I Believe®,* adapted from the international project that engages people in writing and sharing essays describing the core values that guide our daily lives.

Students spent a month discussing and learning about six core values, **Acceptance, Empathy, Hope, Interdependence, Integrity,** and **Pride.** From these core concepts, students explored many other values such as friendship, loyalty, perseverance, laughter, forgiveness, love, and kindness. Students then brainstormed "I believe" statements and listened to, and read, completed essays from various authors posted on the *This I Believe®* website. Finally, students and staff began writing a personal narrative that explains how they came to understand the significance of a core belief. After one week, students and staff turned in a completed essay.

From a student body of 630 students, nearly 95% of students turned in a completed essay. Essays were collected anonymously and students did not receive credit or a letter grade for completing this activity.

All selected essays are published anonymously in this book. Essays were edited for readability and some character names were changed for privacy. A committee consisting of parents and staff selected essays for publication. Staff essays appear at the end of corresponding themed chapters.

I believe everyone is equal. I think people all around the world need to learn how to trust each other, and be honest. When we all learn how to do this, I think our world can come together and make peace. If we learn to trust other people, then we won't have to worry about conflict. Once we do this, we can all start to help our world, and make it a better place.

I don't think anyone is better than anyone else. We are all equal, no matter where we come from, or what color our skin is. We all have a right to stand up for what we believe in. No one has the right to tell someone that what he or she believes is wrong.

I believe we all need to be honest. Whether it's with other people, or with ourselves. I think when we are all honest, then we can begin to trust other people, and know what they are saying is true. It's important to be honest because then you can live your life. No one wants to live a lie.

I believe people need to live, laugh, and love more. We all need to open our hearts and let more people in. We all need to be happy, and live our life to the fullest potential. Everyone can do this with a little trust, honesty, and most importantly, love!

I spend about 32 hours a week at a middle school. A place extremely susceptible to fads and trends, a place filled with people who are acting exactly the same as the person next to them. I believe masking your true self with personalities other than your own creates a life of confusion.

The first day of the school year I was at lunch, and I thought that everyone was either trying to be a skater or a rapper. I feel sorry for my principal, because he remembers everyone's name at my school. But it would be very confusing, because there is a huge group of people who are dressing like Slim Shady. Another large group of people are wearing converse and skinny jeans. It's like everyone is wearing a fad mask. And they are not taking it off, but changing it every few months.

People aren't showing who they really are, and it's creating confusion. This I believe.

I believe in acceptance because it leads to friends. Five years ago I had to change schools. I did not want to leave my friends behind, but I had no choice.

When I got to the school I didn't know anyone, Tthe teacher sent a boy to help me. Everyone was nice to me, and they accepted me into the school. After that school year ended I went back to my old school.

It wasn't as bad as I thought changing schools because I believe in acceptance because it always leads to friends.

For me, acceptance is the most important trait in a person. I don't think people should be judged because of what they watch, listen to, wear, or their style. Everyone is special in his or her own way, and without being yourself everyone would be just like everyone else in the world.

I believe in acceptance because without it everyone would hate or judge each other. In my life I have been judged a lot. I was judged for many things like I wasn't skinny, I was short, ugly, I had messed up teeth, I had weird clothes, ect.... I know this made me feel like crap and I didn't really have friends. One summer I was made fun of by my two best friends, and I cried and sat in my house reading and doing nothing all summer. Whenever I see someone getting made fun of or judged, I try to help out. I try to tell people that are doing it, to stop.

This I believe!

The day seemed like a tragedy, mis-hap, even a bad dream. I believe in acceptance. It set me free from something that kept me locked up.

My parents got a divorce in 2005. On that day, my perfect life came tumbling down. My family and I were devastated.

Moving to Oregon was hardest of all. I felt like we abandoned my dad. We drove away and he faded as we went further.

Days turned to months and months to years. Soon enough we talked about the divorce. They had fallen out of love, and I had to accept it. I believe in acceptance. Sometimes acceptance is the only way to be free!

The first time I walked into middle school, I was so nervous. As the day went by I noticed that none of my friends from elementary school were in any of my classes. I began to feel alone, unwanted, and useless, I just kept quiet for the rest of the day and did what the teachers told me to do. I was like an average, ordinary guy, not a care in the world. The following day I had PE. We had to run a few laps. I just jogged at a pace that I could jog the entire way without slowing down. I met up with a student, he said "Don't I have orchestra with you?" I said "yea." After that we just talked, got to know each other. Then as the day went by I saw him in other classes. I believe in acceptance because it gives you someone to be around and talk too. You don't have to do something to be the center of attention, people accept you for being you!

I always remember heading off to middle school. I was scared and nervous. I didn't know how the other students would act towards me. I was nervous about fitting in, and being myself. I wanted to be liked. I was always worrying about getting my locker open and trying to find the right classes. It's hard being accepted to a new school, there's new people, new teachers, new community, and new rules.

I remember going to my first period class not knowing who would be in there or anything. When I walked into the classroom I felt relieved and excited, I knew tons of people! I was scared for no reason. Everyone was coming up and talking to me, and asking me questions. I felt happy, put into place, loved, and accepted.

Acceptance

In life, people strive for many things. They want success, power, love and plenty more. Throughout elementary school I struggled for what I had wanted most – acceptance. Having very few friends I worked hard to fit in with everyone else. But, a single event, probably a vague memory to others, made me realize what I should have known the moment I first entered school.

In the fifth grade I was nominated for Youth of the Year, a very honorable award. An extravagant banquet was set up and hundreds of people filled the room. Every nominee stood on stage waiting for the one award to be given. As I stood, apprehensive thoughts drowned my mind. I felt like I was on a roller coaster the very moment you're about to drop. Around me, there were outgoing people. They had cell phones and nice clothes. I, on the other hand, was the complete opposite. "Why am I even here"? I kept asking myself. Without a single doubt I was sure I wouldn't get the award.

The moment had come and the presenter's speech was coming to an end. My heart pounded, nervous thoughts still ricocheted in my head. As I listened I slowly heard the speaker utter a name. It took me a few moments to register, but I had won! I was Youth of the Year. The room roared with jubilant cheers as I placed the medal around my neck. Surprisingly, I found myself holding back unexpected tears. As the cheers died down the host continued to say, "she has been a great role model throughout the year. She's smart, motivated and brings joy to the entire school. Unquestionably, she deserves this honor."

When I heard those words, I realized that I was looking for acceptance in the wrong people. I then knew that the true friends I want would recognize my good traits, regardless of my appearance. Now, I look back to that experience and remember to befriend people that are kind and deserving. I believe that acceptance is one of the key fundamentals in life, but you have to want it from the right people.

I believe we shouldn't judge people on outward appearances, true beauty lies on the inside. People often think that beauty out rules feelings. Sometimes people who have beauty think they are better than people who don't. This realization came a few years back when I was in fifth grade.

I was on the bus, going home when I heard people talking about this boy. They were saying how funny his teeth looked, the extra weight on the side of his belt, even the blemishes on his face. Even worse than that, they were talking about it when he was Right There. I wanted to speak up, to tell them to knock it off, but I didn't. I looked at the boy with his flaws, and he was smiling. I won't ever forget that this boy was smiling when he could hear people talk about him so negatively. I'm ashamed of myself for not telling them to stop. I ask myself this, am I any better than them, the ones who made fun of the boy? I can't answer this question myself.

Another time I found myself as the one being made fun of. I'm not overweight, not ugly, nor pretty. I did have a huge flaw though, very bad acne. I still had friends, and they didn't mind the acne. Even though people were nice to me, I did get a few punches to my pride. One time, a boy at my table group said, "wow, Erin, you have tons of pimples!" I blushed in embarrassment. Though my acne is a lot better now, I still feel the hurt of the boy's comment.

Again I notice around school how beauty affects people. At school you see girls wearing as much make-up as they can fit on their face. I feel like I should go up and tell them they look better without the make up, but I doubt they'd believe me.

Beauty is something that people show on the outside, and on the inside. Some people use their beauty as a whip, others keep theirs hidden. This I believe, everyone is beautiful.

I believe in acceptance, because everyone deserves a chance.

My family and I have moved a lot, and it got harder and harder to say goodbye the older I got. Saying "ta-ta" to England was the hardest. We were moving to Oregon. I was 12. At my old school there were no boys and we had to wear uniforms. It was nice because everyone looked the same and no one was fighting over the hot guys.

On my first day of school at HVE, I was anxious, nervous, and a little bit fidgety. I didn't have a uniform, (picking out an outfit was a pain) and there were boys. On top of that my class was going to outdoor school on my third day and I really didn't want to go. I had convinced myself that I wasn't going to make any friends. I remember wishing that I was back in England with my British mates eating a sausage sandwich.

It went a lot better than I thought that it would. I made lots of friends and everyone in my class was kind, but maybe that's because they got to hear a British accent every time I talked. I still miss my UK friends, but I'm very grateful for all of my friends and family that helped me the whole time.

I believe in acceptance, because everyone deserves a chance.

I believe that we shouldn't judge a person by their looks, but what's inside. You should always meet someone new. It doesn't matter if they're different on the outside, what really matters is what's on the inside. We are all the same no matter what.

It all started in third grade. My friends and I were playing in the playground. We were having fun. Then suddenly, I saw a girl getting picked on. I didn't know what to do, but the right thing to do was to tell an adult. The lady came with me as I showed her the way. The boys had to go to the principal's office to call their parents. I helped the little girl get back on her feet, and I asked her if she was alright. She was really shy, and she had a small voice. I couldn't really understand her, but the teacher called her to go into the classroom. I felt really bad for her, because the teacher told me that it was her first day here, and I wanted to welcome her. I thought I could cheer her up as I introduced myself. She told me that her name was Elizabeth, and that it was her first day here, but I already knew that. For the whole school year, Elizabeth and I turned out to be great friends!

A week before summer break, Elizabeth told me that she was moving again! She told me that she's going to see her grandma in Ohio. I was really sad, but I told her that she was a great friend to me and that she would make lots of good friends at her new school.

I believe everyone is different in his or her own way, but we are all the same.

This I believe.

Think back when you were a young kindergartener. At recess you would run down to the sand box and build your sand castles and play around. Other kids start coming your way. Coming to the sandbox. As young as you are, you didn't care what they looked like at all. Even if they were tall, short, skinny or fat. That person was just another friend to play with.

Sadly as we grow older we focus on the outer appearance of people. Never giving them a chance. Just seeing the differences. We don't look for the beauty that lies inside of a person, the true beauty. We judge them on what they wear, how pretty their face is, or how their body is shaped.

True beauty is on the inside, and it's not even hiding from you. It's not the face I love; it's the expressions on it. It's not the voice I love; it's what you say with it. It's not the body I love, it's the way you use it.

I love you for who you are. Can't this world be like that? Can we not see the beauty that lies inside the heart?

Accept their outer beauty no matter what the difference is. Look for the characteristics of a person. Look for the real person inside. Look for the person who treats you well, not for the person with the best clothes. It hurts me to see somebody get treated differently because they do not wear the best clothes, or style their hair everyday.

It makes me feel good inside when I see people bonding with one another. Anger rushes through me when I see a person getting laughed at. Accept people for who they are and love what they really are.

I believe in acceptance because even if you are popular or not, smart or not, you are still unique in your own way.

When I was in 6th grade I made a very bad choice by saying retarded to our valentine bags. Mrs. Nai was passing by and heard me. She said that I was going to be in huge trouble. The Next day Mrs. Nai said that I could help out the kids with severe disabilities in our school. So I said, "ok". The next day I came and helped them over my recess time everyday.

A couple days passed and I started feeling horrible that I called the bags retarded. And I loved coming there, so I asked my best friend Edward if he wanted to help out, and he said, "yes."

The rest of the year we had so much fun and best of all that changed my life forever. I'm glad I went there. I'm sorry for calling those bags retarded and I now know a lot more about people.

I believe it is important for everyone to have acceptance. Everyone in this world should be accepted for who they are. No one should be judged by race, age, or gender, or by how they talk, act or dress.

One big thing people do that's starting to become a problem in schools is stereotyping. Kids have been ignored, left out, and mistreated because of this problem. That's why I think everyone should have acceptance, then it wouldn't become such a problem if everyone in this world could just have a little bit of acceptance.

I believe in a world that is marked by difference, a world that's filled with faces of different colors, backgrounds of different cultures and ideas of different minds. A world where difference is the pinpoint balance between peace and war.

In our world, acceptance is a trait that is commonly shown and both commonly broken. Some people fail to understand another's unique quality, and it leads to discrimination. Discrimination turns into a form of hate, hate transforms into anger, and it all results in human conflicts. There are many good examples of acceptance in this world, but there are inevitably bad ones as well.

A good example of acceptance would be the presidential election and inauguration of Barack Obama. Many believed that Obama had a slight chance of ever reaching his goal due to his color and race, but he defied all odds and was able to push himself to the top. When he was elected president, I have to say that almost everyone in America was accepting on the outside for who Obama was. Those who weren't still have a lot to learn.

A bad example of acceptance would be the Holocaust during World War II. Hitler led Nazis to the idea that the Jews were responsible for the defeat on World War I, and their current economic downfall. He started by singling the Jews out, and that then led to an extermination of an entire race. Over 6 million Jews were lost because of Hitler's foolish action.

A perfect world is what everyone believes in, but we all know that nobody is perfect. However, we can all take a step forward into a better world by accepting others and understanding their differences.

Difference is the only thing that comes between you, your friend, or your teacher. It's the only thing that diversifies us and makes the human race such an interesting species. We must respect them, as much as they respect us. A world in which people were more tolerant of each other is what I believe in.

A lot of people in life are not accepted; others are not accepting. This is a story I am going to share about a time when I was accepting.

Acceptance is when you approve of someone else's rights. Some examples of acceptance are having respect for yourself and others and to not judge others based on looks, rumors, or where they are from.

In sixth grade I went to an open house type thing before the year started, so I could put my supplies in the classroom. I noticed that there were two new girls I had never met before. I felt like saying hello, but I didn't know what the response would be. There were also two boys that I had known for a long time. They showed the girls around the school. At the end of the day I found out the girl's names were Carry and Jenny.

First day of school came and everyone was in their little group except for Jenny. She was on the swings, all by herself. So I went over and started swinging with her. I could tell that she was <u>NOT</u> shy because she just started talking to me. I invited her to come back and hang out with my friends. After recess in the classroom I went and sat by her. Ever since that day we have been best friends!

In seventh grade both of us were busy with sports and homework, but that never stopped us from still being friends. I'll never forget the first day she came to my house. I didn't know what to do. We just sat in my bedroom and now, there is never enough time to finish everything.

That day I learned an important lesson. No matter what they look like, or what people say about them, that

Acceptance 23

person deserves a chance. That day I gave Jenny a chance and we became great friends.

Acceptance is what I believe.

I believe in acceptance. At my old school everyone wanted to be a part of the "popular group." I didn't though.

The definition of popular group is kids who only think about themselves. One day my friend wanted to be a part of the "popular group," so she went and asked, "can I join your group?" and guess what they said? NO because they thought only of themselves.

It is not how popular you are or what group you're in that counts, it's friends and acceptance. I told my friends, "you guys are always accepted in my group." No matter what, everyone is accepted.

I believe in acceptance, and that everyone is equal. This is why I believe in acceptance. No matter what happens I always will.

I believe in equality because no matter how big or small, old or young everyone should be treated the same.

When I was seven my dad passed away, and my mom decided to move. When my mom told me we were moving I was happy and devastated at the same time. She told me that this was my last weekend in Westport, and that I can spend it with anyone I wanted. So, I decided that I wanted to spend it with Marisa!

It was around December, and we went to her dad's house. When we woke up the next day, her dad asked us what we wanted to do. Marisa left it up to me. I asked her dad if we could go to the docks, and he nodded his head. We got our bathing suits and lifejackets. He packed a lunch and we hopped in his pick-up truck.

When we got there, Marisa and I looked sheepishly at the piling docks. We had seen them before, but usually we saw the older kids on them. We looked at each other, and smiled. We ran back to Marisa's dad and asked if we could jump off the pilings. He looked at us and said "Bayleigh, Marisa this is your last time to do this together, so....go for it!" We ran giggling back to the pilings, crawled on top holding hands and counted to three. The first time we both chickened out, but the second time we both jumped. At first it felt like I was flying; then I thought we were going to die. Then we hit the water and surfaced. I knew that I would never again be afraid of the pilings.

I now know that when you only have one more shot at something life will let you have a try.

Everyone should be treated the same and this is why I believe in equality.

Second grade seemed like such a long time ago. Everything was fine, I was normal – as normal as any seven year old could be, but things changed. My mother sensed that something was wrong when I didn't respond after she had already said my name five times, so she brought me to the Hearing and Speech Institute.

After many days of testing and long hours of waiting, they finally started giving us answers. There was indeed something wrong with me. I qualified for hearing aids. Because I was so young I didn't know what to think; I was confused, frustrated by the waiting and angry with myself for not noticing earlier. That wasn't the worst of it though.

By the time another year had passed I had to go back for my annual check-up. They found something new. My hearing levels had dropped, and after three more years it dropped again. I thought to myself, was there something horribly wrong with me? Why did this happen to me? Well, they came up with some answers. My hearing was going to get lower every year, and that, eventually, at a certain age I was going to lose it all. I was going to be deaf.

I can't tell you how many times I cried about it. People would treat me different, they didn't understand. They would get so annoyed with me because I couldn't hear what they were saying. Some people thought that I was ignoring them. That only made it worse. My friends grew scarce. It wasn't until then, I realized that the ones who still stayed by my side, despite the burden I was carrying, were the only ones that mattered. There were so many times when I tried to convince myself that losing my hearing every year was good, but I kept coming up empty handed, blind to the normal things in life.

By the time I was in fifth grade I moved to another school. I was a buddy for this little girl who had Down Syndrome. Seeing Emma smile changed me. She inspired me. She had Down Syndrome, but yet, she was the happiest kid I've ever known. I had to stop drowning myself in self-pity. I was not going to let it slow me down.

I could have dreams of being a writer, musician, or something else crazy. I was still going to use the time I had left. Nobody should just stop because they have dyslexia. No one should mope around and think that they're worthless because the have ADHD. People with disabilities should let nothing slow them down and let their stories inspire everyone, everywhere. This I believe.

I believe in acceptance of the way people are. Acceptance is important to people in different ways. Some people want to be accepted, while other people think it is important to accept others. Before seventh grade, I was in the first group, but after the first week of seventh grade, I moved into the second group of people. The awakening I had during that first week of seventh grade changed my whole thought process.

In sixth grade, a new boy (who's name I won't say) came to Happy Valley Elementary and ended up in my class. At the beginning of the year I didn't talk to him very much. When I did talk to him, I thought he was really annoying. I also thought he was weird because he was unique. He started off sixth grade without any friends.

As sixth grade moved on, everyone was being rude and mean to him. People looked for any mistakes he made. Somehow, he didn't let the criticism bother him. The boy still greeted me every time I saw him. Of course I didn't notice this until I saw him some time during the first week of seventh grade.

I was on my way to my locker, when I saw the boy. He didn't say "hi" or anything, he just walked past me. I suddenly realized that the first time he hadn't said "hello" to me was at that moment. I felt terrible about the things I'd done because he was a good person that got made fun of. Since that day, I've greeted him every time I seen him, and he has returned the greeting with a SMILE.

The boy changed my beliefs from trying to be cool, to accepting people for the way they are. He had always been nice to me. Now, I'm always nice to him. He changed my life and my beliefs. I believe in acceptance of the way people are.

When I walk the halls of my school, I try to greet everyone I see and be as kind to everyone as I possibly can. For me, this is a big surprise to be so outgoing when I think that only five years before, I was out on a playground and looking for someone to at least acknowledge my presence. I was the new kid in the school, and I had become very shy during the move, making me an unsociable third grader.

I was scared that I would be rejected. I stayed out of everyone's way and never asked if I could play with them or sit down at a lunch table beside someone. My friends at Sunnyside Elementary left me with good thoughts and encouragement at the end of second grade, but their reassurances were meaningless now that I was at my new school (Happy Valley Elementary) and facing my second-worst fear: having no friends. Before I moved, my parents signed me up for Girl Scouts, and those girls were the only people I knew in my new school. For some reason, I was scared to talk to them at school, leaving me alone on the light-colored bark chips. Every recess, I would walk around the playground, watching everyone else have fun doing the activities they do. At one point, I noticed a swing set in the distance. I loved swinging and jumping off of the swing at the highest point (at my old school), but here, the swing set was so huge to me, I dared not get closer. In the middle of the playground next to the slides, there was a dome with brightly colored hexagons scattered on the outside, connecting the many bars that crisscrossed and made up the outside of the dome. After a week of just shuffling around and doing nothing, I sat on one of the bars of the dome and watched people pass me by. In the distance, I saw a girl about my age walking in the general direction of me. Thinking she would just walk by, I looked back down at my shoes. I heard the girl getting closer and then stop. Glancing up, I saw her right in front of me.

"Hi! I'm Anna. What's your name?" she asked me eagerly. Startled, I told her my name, and that I was the new kid. Intrigued, Anna asked why I wasn't playing. I responded with the simplest answer I could: "I have no friends." She told me that if no one would be friends with me, then we'd just have to make friends. Through the rest of the year, Anna and I were very good friends and we played every day with the imaginary pets we harbored in our minds. Anna accepted who I was, in spite of me being new and practically a stranger to everyone. Acceptance: this is what I believe in.

Four years ago a decision impacted my life and changed the life of another.

I sat swinging my legs back and forth trying to hold back tears of sympathy as I gazed at the tragic pictures the screen projected. I stumbled in my train of thought. Seeing those poor faces pushing through struggles no one should go through. Poverty. Loss. Hunger. And to believe they still have abundant hope at the end of the day. At that moment I knew I had to do something, something that could help someone, and I acted on it. In my world everywhere I look I can find a reason to be thankful.

Poverty fills the land. Imagine, no food for days, no fresh water, no medical care, imagine supporting a family you can't afford. Everyday is a struggle to survive for these wonderful people. Your life is a luxurious fantasy to the citizens that live in this impoverished country. Unfortunately problems similar to this fill the world or even our own cities.

I now sponsor a young boy named Nkosiyazi from a small country in South Africa, called Swaziland. I receive monthly letters with pictures from Nkosiyazi thanking me and my family for giving him opportunities he would otherwise not have. We have helped his village build a small school the size of a small bedroom, provided them the education and tools to harvest corn, helped build a small irrigation system and a water pump with a well where the village children are no longer at risk from adult predators as they seek for water holes to carry water back to the village. Even something as simple as medical care is not available to Nkosiyazi and his village.

Every month we receive a letter and picture of Nkosiyazi, smiling from ear to ear and ever so thankful for the little items that my friends and I have always taken for granted; Crayola crayons, a note pad, a throw blanket, socks, stickers and pencils. Reading his letters makes me happy to know that I am making a difference to his life.

An act of kindness needs not be something big and showy, it can be as simple as holding a door open, giving a smile, or treating others kindly and respectfully regardless of appearance.

A common saying is: "Be kind to your neighbor." In our day-to-day life this motto begins to dim, like a dying star. We discriminate and criticize individuality and other traits in life that seem "odd." I believe that we should embrace the differences of others and treat them with kindness. An act of kindness can greatly impact someone's life; it's the key to changing the lives of millions. This I believe.

    I believe that everybody needs to treat people as they wanted to be treated. Once when I moved to another school, kids did bad stuff to me like calling me names and spreading rumors about me. At that school I didn't have a lot of friends because of the popular girl. Everything was getting worse. People started pushing me and getting me in trouble for nothing.

    When my teacher asked what was going on, I told her the story and the popular girl got in trouble. Then one of her best friends became my friend, so I got a lot of friends and the popular girl didn't have any friends. One week later she came up to me and said that she was sorry about everything. I told her "just let's be friends but you have to remember one thing, 'treat people as you want to be treated.'" I think it's important because if you want to hurt someone's feelings or do something bad you have to think, do I want to be in that situation first and then do it.

I believe in acceptance. When I was seven years old, acceptance was the exact opposite of what was happening. Every day I would sit at the same table with all my friends and the only thing that they could talk about was how weird and different this girl was. They would crack jokes about her because she was different when she talked. From the outside she looked completely normal to everyone else, but my friends couldn't get over the fact that she can't talk. Every day this girl would sit by herself. She had no one to talk to and no one to laugh with. And last year when she invited us all to her birthday, no one came, including me. I felt sorry for her even though I know she didn't want me to. The girl had never bothered anyone so my friends had no right to make fun of her.

I was so tired of hearing all the mean jokes about her, so I got up and walked over to her. When I got there, I picked up all her stuff and brought her to our table. She told me that her name was Samantha in sign language. All my other friends scooted to the end of the table, so I said a funny joke and she felt better. We have been best friends ever since.

Acceptance, this I believe.

Acceptance

I believe that without acceptance we would not be able to survive as a community. A community has many different social groups. As a community we must learn to accept each group so that we do not result in failure as a community.

During my brother's freshman and sophomore years of high school, he participated in wrestling. His freshman wrestling career was great, but unfortunately his sophomore year wasn't. As his sophomore wrestling career wore on he began to get picked on by the entire team, eventually losing the acceptance of the team. The team started excluding him and making fun of him. Eventually my brother grew tired of the disrespect and he quit wrestling even though he was a good wrestler and he was close to receiving his letter.

Later that year I started wrestling. I enjoyed the sport so much that I would walk over to the high school and wrestle off-season practices with the high-schoolers. Over time they started to like me. I fit in and they accepted me. It was a bitter sweet feeling because I was happy for myself but sad for my brother.

Seeing my accomplishment, my brother grew to hating wrestling. He wouldn't show me moves and he didn't want to go to my meets. He avoided the wrestling world as much as possible. I believe that as a community we must learn to accept each other because if we don't the community will fall apart and we will lose each other.

    I believe in acceptance. Accepting people for who they are, accepting the world for what it has become, and accepting life for what it is destined to be. There are so many different types of personalities in the world, but who really cares what they wear or how they act? We are all people and we don't need to go on judging a person on their size, shape, or color. None of that should matter; don't judge a book by its cover. Open it up and read what's inside. If you don't judge you won't be judged.

    I think back to first, second, and even third grade; where I was friends with everyone and everyone was friends with me, now it just seems so complicated. Everybody has their stupid clicks that they hang with. If you're not in that click you're the enemy? I don't quite get that whole theory. The way I see it, people are way too judgmental. For myself I try to be a part of all the "clicks." To me it doesn't matter what others think. Friends are something to value, and if you got their back they'll have yours. In my mind, the definition of a true friend is someone who will laugh with you, cry with you and travel to the moon with you if that's what it takes to help get you through life.

Last year I was going through a major speed bump in my life where my parents were separated and were seriously talking the big "D" Divorce. My mind was all over the place and I wasn't always the same person that my friends knew. I was so confused and angry that I just kind of shut the whole world out and hated my parents for what they were doing. Something that really helped me through all of that was my church group. They helped me get through the thick and thin of my times. They accepted me for who I was and they helped me become a better person. Acceptance has truly been a part of my life from the beginning and I hope that it can become a part of everyone's life because all people aren't the same but we all appreciate being accepted by the others in this world.

I believe that acceptance strengthens the bond of a community.

    I believe in acceptance. I believe in acceptance because acceptance is realizing and knowing everyone and everything is different from each other, and accepting that. People go their whole life being judged by others for the way they are. They are judged instead of being accepted for who they are. We as people, thrive to be accepted by other people, or a certain group of people, because I think it is a natural instinct to want to fit in with everyone else, and be loved and cared for. In school, I think it's even harder to be accepted because we have these "clicks" of people and some are less accepting than others. In my opinion, acceptance is very important. This I believe.

I believe that acceptance is a big part of your 7th grade year. When I was in 7th grade I felt like I didn't fit in anywhere. At school it was hard to make new friends. Every day when it started I wanted it to be over. Then my dad said drop the show and just be yourself. The next day I went to school myself and things changed. Then I figured it out, people want to be around a person that is true to themselves. I made some great new friends that year. I think we will be friends for years to come. What I'm trying to say is don't change for everyone or anything. Stay true to who you are. Trust me, I've been through the things you are in or are about to go through. The best thing I did was be myself. Before I was myself I was trying so hard to fit in with the popular kids but it never worked. Remember that it doesn't matter if you're the richest in the school or the poorest in the school. People will accept you if you stay true to who you are.

I believe in acceptance. What goes around comes around. Without acceptance, there would be no relationships, countries, families, or friends. The world would be at war with one another. When I was 13 years old at Sunrise Middle School in P.E. I learned how important acceptance is. It was scooter racing day; one of the most competitive activities in P.E. Like most 7th graders, I wanted to be the very best. So I had to pick the very best team. I ended up choosing my best friend Tracy, and another kid who looked pretty athletic. Thinking I had the best group, we took a seat. Then one of the P.E. teachers came up to our group and said we needed one more person. I started looking for all the people that I knew were athletic, but they were all in a group. I then saw one boy who had no group, and seemed very shy. I asked if he wanted to join our group, and he was very happy to. During the scooter races, we ended up in last place, but I didn't care. I had made a new friend by accepting him into our group, and we have been friends ever since. Even though he wasn't the most athletic person. When I think back on this day, it makes me proud. Acceptance isn't the easiest thing to do, and I know that now. I want people to know before this event happened, I was really, really competitive. I thought nothing could be better than winning, but I was wrong. Now I know that it doesn't matter if someone isn't like you and doesn't enjoy the same things as you do like sports. It's about making friendships and accepting who they are as a person. As I said acceptance is huge. It makes me who I am today. To know that everyone has their strengths and flaws, including myself, and accepting me for who I am as a person. It is what I most believe in, and what I always will believe in because how you treat people is how people will treat you.

    I believe that people should not be judged on what they wear and their ethnicity. It is not fair just to be called uncool by what you wear or what ethnicity you are. I have been blamed of doing bad things that I actually never did just because I'm categorized as "Ukrainian/Russian." People think we are all troublemakers just because of our ethnicity. It is pretty close to being racist. I believe it is unfair to be judged this way because I'm different than other people. Just because I'm not the coolest or most popular person in school does not give anyone the right to treat me in such a bad way. I've seen this with many other groups that are put down because of their ethnicity. I believe that people should not be judged by what they wear or who they are. I have been called names for wearing certain clothing. I didn't take it to mind, but to someone else it could be seriously offensive. This I believe.

When I moved and changed schools for the first time, I was very scared. I just didn't know what to expect, and in my mind I was constantly thinking about how things could go wrong or if the kids would be really mean. But I knew I had to do it and it was only 4th grade, so I took on the task of going to a new school for the first time with confidence.

The very first day was great. Everybody was very welcoming, but after a couple more days people's true personality came into play. It was then I could see who my real friends were—a group of hyper boys who just wanted to have a good time. I'm still friends with them today.

What I found at that point is that you have to accept it when things don't go exactly how you want it to. I didn't want to move, I didn't want to switch schools, and I didn't want to interact with the kids there, but I had to accept that that is the way things work and everything turned out fine. To become successful you have to accept your problems and continue on anyways. This I believe.

I believe in many things. I believe in God. I believe that war is not the solution to anything. I believe that everyone should be honest. I believe that everyone can have their own beliefs, and they should not be judged by their beliefs. One simple thing I believe in is acceptance. There is one amazing person that made me believe in acceptance.

It was the beginning of my third grade school year, but it wasn't just any regular first day of school. I had just moved from Gresham to Happy Valley, and now I was going to a brand new school that I had never seen before.

I walked into class with my purple backpack and my Lisa Frank pencil case that was full of all my freshly sharpened #2 pencils. I had butterflies in my stomach and I anxiously looked around at all the unfamiliar faces. I slowly walked towards the desk that had my name on it and sat down. Most of the tables were in groups of four, but mine was in a group of five.

Before I knew it, the teacher, Mrs. Norton, was telling us to gather in a circle on the floor. Once we were all in a circle, well it wasn't really a circle, but more of a lumpy jellybean shape, Mrs. Norton began to talk again. She explained that we were going to go around in a circle and introduce ourselves. We would also name an animal that started with the same letter as our name. Instantly, I became nervous. It was just a silly little game, but I wasn't looking forward to speaking in front of the class at all.

The first person began to speak, and then the next person, and the next. Pretty soon, it was the person right before me who was speaking.

"Hi, I'm Destiny," the girl said in a little voice. "An animal that starts with the same letter as my name is dog."

"Hi, I'm Taylor," I said in a quivery voice. "An animal that starts with a letter "t" like my name is turtle."

Just like that, my turn was over. I was very relieved. The rest of the students introduced themselves, and after they were done, Mrs. Norton began to speak. "Good job. Everyone did great. Now, we have a new student at this school. Her name is Taylor. Would anyone like to be a buddy for her?"

Immediately, the girl next to me, Destiny, raised her hand. Mrs. Norton picked her.

"Thank you, Destiny," Mrs. Norton continued, "all you will need to do is show Taylor around and help her at lunch and recess."

I was very thankful for this wonderful friend. Destiny showed me around, helped me meet many new people, and she just made me feel so comfortable. Without Destiny, my third grade year wouldn't have started well. Although I didn't know it at the time, Destiny and I would become very good friends for many years to come.

I believe that anyone is willing to accept people. It is just that sometimes they aren't brave enough to, and they feel that if they accept someone new, their other friends will get upset. Even with this possibility, Destiny stepped up and offered to help me. I really appreciate her, and I will never forget what she did for me.

Acceptance is one of those words that can sometimes mean a lot to someone. It's one of those words that when it's used, it could affect someone greatly. The word acceptance has made a large impact on me.

When I was eight years old, I transferred to a different school because of my mom's job. I had to transfer from a private school to a public school, which was very different for me. Transferring to a public school meant no more uniforms so I had to get used to that. I had to say goodbye to all my friends, my teachers, and everyone else that was there. But on the bright side, I thought I could make new friends at this new school I was going to.

On my first day of public school, I was completely lost on what to do and where to go. Kids were looking at me like I was from another planet. From that point on, I thought that I would never fit in.

When I entered the classroom that I was put in, I was embarrassed. Everyone stared at me again. The class was in the middle of a reading group activity and the teacher told me to join any group of my choice. I looked around and was hesitant to join every group I looked at. Then instead of me asking, somebody else asked if I wanted to join their group. Everyone introduced themselves and they made me feel like they were my friends from the beginning, and plus they really did say they were my friends.

True acceptance takes more than words to mean it. It takes heart to mean it. I believe that acceptance is important in life.

I believe in being yourself. This I believe because when I was about 13-1/2 I didn't have many friends. But one day during the second trimester in Spanish and math class, I was sitting next to two girls, and that day I was being myself. I was being goofy, crazy, funny and weird. Then I said something funny, I guess, because the girls started laughing, and I felt happiness and joy in my heart because we then started talking and became friends. But, before this event, I felt alone and different from everyone else because I do very unusual things. Now I know that being myself will let others know who I really am. Values I thought were, and are still today, important are trust, being outgoing and honesty. So I believe in being yourself because it is the best way to make new friends. Also, it is an honest way of showing who you really are to others.

I believe everyone should be treated fairly. No matter what they look like, short, tall, fat, or skinny. My best friend, Emily, and I were walking down the street to her house, when I lived in California. We went up to her new neighbors and Emily said hi and told them her name. They responded, "We don't want to hang out with a fat person!" Once Emily heard that, she ran home crying. I didn't know what to do; we were only seven. I remember every time I would see her I would think about that day. She always got teased for being overweight, but the next year I moved away to Oregon. Whenever I would go to visit her she would get teased and I never knew what to do, but the next year I went down her mom said she had made some bad decisions with drugs and drinking and they had sent her to a rehab center for a year in Bend, Oregon, but would be better and home by the next year I came. Last year I went again and they had said she came home and made it worse. They told me they sent her to a drug and drinking rehab school in Phoenix, Arizona. I asked when she would be back and they didn't know. They said in the next year or two. It really hit me then how bad some things can hurt people and that by just a few people saying something can change a person's life forever. This has really taught me not to say things that might hurt people even if you are just kidding. I can't wait to see her again. I haven't seen her in years. After this happened, though it made me realize how big of a problem teasing is in the world, that it's not a joking thing, it can be very serious.

Acceptance

I believe no matter what someone looks like, underweight, overweight, tall, short, brown hair, blond hair, red hair, anything, we should all be treated equally.

I believe that every person should be equal and that the only person you will always need to impress is yourself. Two weeks and 1 year ago I found that out for myself. We were at my parent's friends house for a birthday party.

Everyone referred to one another as sir. It felt awkward being the youngest there, at age 13. I was not only the youngest but the smallest. For the longest time I had thought that the way to earn my title as sir, I would have to do something impressive, something that everyone would treat you differently for for the rest of my life. I had always wanted to be seen as equal.

That night I talked in one of my longest conversations with one of the wisest people I know. We talked for what seemed like an eternity and yet it was only a half hour. I had found out more about him in that half hour than I had of anyone. Our conversation consisted of many topics, school, future colleges, and sports. We somehow stumbled onto the topic of equality. We talked about how when he was a kid it was still somewhat frowned upon for a white man to marry a black woman or vice versa. I asked him when people started treating him as an adult. He said, "when does not matter, but how is what counts." I asked him how, he said, "when someone saw me do the right thing when no one was looking." Then I realized that impressing people is not how they are going to treat you equal, but the things you do when no one is looking and how you do it to impress yourself is when it counts. If I had not learned that that day, I probably would still be showing off trying to impress people to better myself.

Acceptance

That is my way of becoming equal. People may or may not like it, that's not for me to decide but for people to decide for their own. When you become equal is not your choice in an adult's eye, but how is all that adults and you remember.

    I believe everybody is different. Being different is a good thing. We should honor the looks and traits God has given us. When I was in 4th grade, I had made new friends. Their names were Megan, Kayla, and Emily. Everybody knew them, and I wanted to be like them. I wanted to be known. So after hanging out with them, I started dressing like them. And after that, I started talking like them. All four of us looked and talked the same. We were like clones. I spent most of my time looking in a mirror or looking through my clothes. After a week, I finally realized that I wasn't myself. What I was doing was wrong. I thought about it all weekend. When Monday came, I apologized to my old friends right away. I told them that I was just being foolish. I explained that I was so jazzed about getting a chance to be like Megan, Kayla, and Emily. I just forgot who I really was. So in the end, my true best friends and I made up and I was still friends with Megan, Kayla, and Emily. I learned that you shouldn't change yourself for anybody, not even for being known. If you be yourself, then you will always have friends. This I believe.

I believe in creativity and acceptance because anyone who looks or acts different shouldn't be bullied or shunned for their actions. Instead they should be admired for their skills and respected for who they are. When I went to my grade school one day, I noticed something different. There was a new student to the school. He was kind of shy at first. I would be to if I was a new student because you don't know a single soul. I decided to talk to this new student. He didn't say much at first, but after awhile I started to realize that he was a really skilled person. He's a great artist, kind, and the funniest person you would have ever known. There is nothing wrong with being different. People should accept people who are different. In fact, most of the famous scientists acted different. For example, did you know Albert Einstein didn't know how to tie his own shoes until he was 20. Another example would be Thomas Edison. People thought he was unteachable because he didn't pay attention in any of his classes, but look at him now he's the guy who invented the light bulb. And Albert, without him we wouldn't know anything about $E=mc2$ or the structure of atoms. Don't make fun of people who act or look different instead admire them. I believe in creativity and acceptance.

    I believe in acceptance because people should accept others for who they are, not for how they look, talk or act. This has happened to me many times before. When I first moved here I was alone. I had no friends at all. People were also constantly teasing me because I was short, skinny, and couldn't pronounce my "r's" and I still can't. My life stayed like this all the way up until the end of the 6th grade when I made my first true friend here. He was able to get past all of my weird traits and get to know me for who I really was. He accepted me not by my looks or traits, but for the person I really was. Him and I are still best friends and probably always will be.

I believe it is wrong to treat people different than the others. From their size, looks, or even how they are born. It's wrong because they are the same as you on the inside.

Over the years I have seen bullying, teasing, and left out students. I try to keep them in and those who treat them badly out. I know I am doing better than those who tease because I treat others the way I want to be treated. It hurts to hear my best friends laugh at others. When I hear that I just walk away and hope they would never do it again.

I have once myself been treated as if I had something wrong with me. I was left out and I have been for an entire year. So I always put me in their position and think positive about myself.

I believe it is wrong to treat people different than others.

I believe in acceptance and how it is important for everyone to be accepted for who they are. I didn't really put much thought into people being accepted before I saw that my own peers were getting teased just because they're a little different than others. Now I believe that everyone needs acceptance in their life.

In my first period Spanish class, last trimester, there was this 7th grade guy that would always choose to sit in the back of the classroom. Almost everyday he would try to grab everyone's attention by talking loud, asking out of topic questions, and tilting his desk. And once he snuggled his whole body inside his shirt. But hey, he's still a person and it doesn't give anyone a right to criticize him.

I was out in the hallway after lunch and I spotted four or five people crowding my Spanish class peer. I overheard them trying to make him do something to get attention. I felt shocked and disappointed in how they were treating him like a performing monkey! He's a person and he has feelings. They don't know how hurt my classmate must've been.

Being present to watch my peer getting teased and in the spotlight which he probably didn't want to be in was surprising. I would've never suspected that some people could be that cruel. But I knew after awhile that I had to see it. For I will see it once again in the future. I saw that everyone, it doesn't matter what size, shape, race, culture they have, but everyone needs acceptance in life. We all are different form each other. So we all need to be accepted. This I believe.

In third grade I had to move. I knew why we had to move, I thought it was a good reason. But I didn't want to leave my friends. I believe that you have to accept what happens and move on.

My parents decided to move when I was in third grade so I had time to make new friends before middle school. The middle school in the Centennial district was horrible. There were gangs and fights in the school everyday. On the last day of third grade, my friends and I all started crying. I did not want to go.

In the fall school started and I was completely reluctant to go. I saw a person from my old school and felt more comfortable. Eventually I made more friends and was used to my new school.

I just had to accept that I was going to a new school. I had to accept that I had to leave my friends and remember it's easy to make friends. I believe you have to accept what happens and move on.

I believe in acceptance because we should be accepted for who we are. When I was seven, in first grade, I was picked on for speaking a different language. I was shy and really quiet. Every day when I came home from school, I would go to my room, close the door, and cry. I always said "Why me, why me?" My parents couldn't take it any more, so we moved. Here in Happy Valley I was accepted by students that were different from me. So what if your skin color is different, and you speak another language. It doesn't matter. Others can learn an important lesson from one another, that's because not everyone is the same. Also remember no one is perfect. Just like everyone else.

Acceptance

My belief is acceptance for something as simple as a half of a soccer game. I was 8 years old at the Spring Mountain soccer field when the half time whistle blew. Everyone had a position accept for me when our goalie said he wasn't feeling good so I had to take his place. I was ready to kick some butt as goalie because I had practiced a little before the game but I wasn't so sure because my normal position was defense. The game was going good until the ball started coming my way. I missed shot after shot and I could feel my face becoming red. I was thinking I was letting everybody down by being so bad and I felt so demoralized that I wanted to cry. When the game was finally over the score was 15 to 8. That's how bad I did. The funny thing was nobody cared that I had done so suckish. They were just happy I gave it my all. I thought, "wow, it must have taken a lot to be okay with losing when we had the game in the bag." I still look back to that day and look back at the acceptance they showed for me. That's why it's okay to have acceptance.

    I believe that everyone has value and that everyone is the same. I believe in acceptance. Everyone should be accepted how they are and in what they believe. When I came to America I was feeling left out all the time. At lunch I was always alone. It seemed like no one liked me. Everyone had friends to talk to but I had just myself. There are times when you need to tell someone but there's no one. After awhile a girl came up to me and asked if I wanted to play. I said, "yes". Later, we became friends. I wish our school wasn't like that, but welcomed everyone. Even if they have a different religion, I still think everyone is important, and mean something. I believe that everyone has value and everyone is the same.

Acceptance

I believe accepting people for who they are is one of the best gifts you can give to another person. From experience, I know what it's like to be left out of everything at school, to be talked about behind my back just because I didn't look the same as everybody else. It was the hardest thing to get over in my life. This all happened to me when I was a 9 year old young girl just enjoying what life had to offer. I never took things for granted until this horrendous accident occurred in my life. I was run over by a parade float on the fourth of July, 2005. I was rushed to the hospital by helicopter, uncontious, not knowing how my life would be different. I had injuries I couldn't understand or even focus about over the pain I was feeling. I had my whole right rib cage shattered with dislocated, broken ribs. My face had broken bone throughout my cheeks and eyes and of course, my jaw. I lost my two front teeth, they were gone forever. My lung has a hole in it that will stay with me til the day that I die. I couldn't believe I was still alive, seeing and speaking the same I was before. I could not believe it, and I still can't.

Seven days passed of a long, endless amount of pain throughout myself. I returned to my normal life unexpectedly fast, and I wasn't ready for all that was going to happen. Months passed with no front teeth and a face of a monster. School was absolutely hell. Everywhere I turned people were staring or whispering to their friends. All I had was my family and people who were truly there for me. All I wanted was to be accepted, accepted for me and to be understood for my story, a piece of my life that will haunt me forever. Today, I know what it's like to feel you're not important, but life will amaze you with people who are real and accept you for who you are. This I believe.

I believe in acceptance. I think that all people should accept others, even if all your friends don't want you to, or the person is just really weird. When I see someone being left out, I will go over and include them in what we are doing.

A few weeks ago, my boy scout troop was on a campout. We had just arrived and we were getting into groups of three's for our tents. I found one partner quickly and then I saw one boy who is normally left out of activities and groups. He was being told by everyone else that they didn't want him in their tent. This bothered me a little. So my buddy and I both walked over to this one boy and asked him if he wanted to stay in our tent with us. He gladly accepted our invite.

When I see these kinds of things going on, I try and fix it. I hate excluding people because they're different. I wish that nobody would exclude others. I wish that everybody could learn to accept anybody. This would make people like the boy in my troop, to feel a lot more welcome in larger groups of people. Accepting others is very big for me, and that's why I believe in acceptance.

I believe in many things. I feel that diverse beliefs make people unique. I believe that accepting others for who they are is an important part of who I am. Most of my friends are like myself. We play sports together and get along great. It was a little different with my other friend. He didn't play sports. He didn't wear Nike shocks or Adidas shorts. This story is an example of accepting people for who they are.

I was in second grade. The sun was shining and there was no school. It was a perfect day to do to the park and play basketball with my friends. This all changed when I got a phone call from my friend. It was my friend who was a little different, a little weird. He asked me to the movies with him. I didn't want to go. I wanted to play basketball. I thought about asking him to play basketball instead. He wouldn't want to do that though. It wasn't that I didn't like him, I just felt a little weird around him, kind of embarrassed. I didn't want to hurt his feelings though, so I decided to accept his invite.

I ended up having a great time at the movies. His mom even took us out for pizza afterwards. It sure beat basketball at the park. I learned I had a lot more in common with this friend than I thought.

I believe accepting others for who they are is important.

Acceptance

    I believe that acceptance is the true remedy for sorrow. I was nine, I was diagnosed with legg-calve-perthes syndrome. Legg-calve-perthes syndrome is a degenerative disease of the hip joint. I was told that I could not put any pressure on my right leg for two years, unless I was in the water. I could not play any sport unless it was swimming. When I learned that there was an activity I could do to be normal, I quickly joined. To my surprise, I was very good at swimming. When I was in the water, it made me feel normal. One of my teammates was shocked when I got out of the water and used my crutches. Over those past two years, I was confused, jealous and alone. I did not understand why or how it happened to me. I envied my peers who were able to use their legs. Being the only one in my class with crutches, I felt like an outcast. I found myself looking for answers. I passed a classroom with disabled students like me, but I could not help but understand how they felt. I caught myself passing the classroom and sneaking glimpses at the special education class. I began to understand how lucky I am. I couldn't possibly imagine how much pain they've endured and how much strength they have. I learned from them and that changed my life forever. I learned that I should accept anyone who comes my way and accept those who have not harmed you. Ignore those who have. Don't judge others by how they look, because everyone deserves acceptance. I believe that acceptance is the true remedy for sorrow.

  I believe that all people are equal and should all be accepted. I believe in acceptance because I was shown this at a time in my life when I was in the third grade. Everything was going perfectly. I had good friends, teachers and support. By the time it was near the end of the year my parents told us we would be moving. At the time I was super excited and ready. But, as time passed I realized how frightening it was for me to leave all I have. I thought of all other negatives like what if no one likes me because I'm weird or stupid. By the time I realized I wasn't ready it was too late. The deal had closed and we were moving to Happy Valley. The first day of the 4th grade had to be the hardest. I was in a school community where everyone knew each other and were already in groups. I found myself alone and enclosed from everyone else. Those were very lonely and heartbreaking days. Soon after that, I realized that just one person can make all the difference. I was out on recess one sunny day, walking alone like usual. When a boy came over and invited me to the swings with him. This made me realize that even though he didn't know me, he had the courage to accept me into his group. This made me compelled to do the same. I started getting out more, making new friends and feeling a part of something. I thought deep and hard about the courage that boy took and it really changed my life. I learned to accept people for who they are not who I want them to be. That boy gave me a sense of hope. He gave me interdependence and without that I would never be who I am today. For that I believe in accepting people for who they are because all people are equal.

Acceptance

I believe that we have the courage to do anything. I had the courage to move to Florida and attend a new school. The day my mom told me I was moving to Florida with my dad was very sad because I did not really want to go.

When I was ten years of age, I was diagnosed with turrets. Turrets is a form of ADHD. So something like going to a new school was hard. I was crying every night till I moved.

I didn't want to go. First, I didn't want to leave my friends, and two, I didn't want to get teased about my turrets. A few weeks later, I was all packed and ready to move. Soon enough I was in Florida. I got all moved in and ready for school.

I was the new girl. I meet so many kids and meet lots of friends. About six weeks later, everyone found out that I have turrets. So, everyone started teasing me. I lost some friends and kept some friends. My best friend Abby was still my friend, but not my best friend. I remember going home after school and not tell my dad anything about all the teasing.

I really did not like being teased all the time. Awhile later people realized that my turrets was not that bad. I made more friends, but still some teased me. I wanted everyone to stop teasing me, so I had to find the courage to stand up for myself. Once I found the courage I stood up for myself, I gained more friends.

Courage

I believe in courage. The courage to do anything you put your mind too. I feel all of this has made me a better person. The end!

Everyday people everywhere are succeeding at their goals. Although, quite a few people are giving up their goals because they think that they aren't able to achieve them. Or, people begin to think that they aren't good enough. I think differently. I believe everyone has value.

It was the final soccer game in the tournament and I grew more nervous by the second. My team was tied for first place. I watched my team's defense fight their hardest to keep away the intruders from the other team. Towards the end, the whistle blew and it was a tied game. It came down to PK's.

I watched each player from my team and the other miss their shots. I began to see a pattern. Finally, someone made it. It was my turn and the game was tied. I prepared my shot and kicked with all my power at the goal. It went in! I ran back to screaming girls and we got first place!

That day, I learned that people should never doubt themselves. People can do anything if they believe in themselves. I believe everyone has value, no matter what!

Courage

Courage is something I cherish and believe in. Why I believe in courage is because, there was once a moment that I experienced when I was worried, scared, terrified, and fearful. I believe in courage because courage is facing a difficulty even though it may be dangerous or painful. Courage is bravery. You should always try even though you may have been unsuccessful in the past. Without courage you couldn't be successful and reach your goals.

I believe in courage because one day on a field trip we went hiking. We went hiking to the big famous tree of Camp Magruder. When I say big, I mean it! The tree was huge! It had a thick long rope tied to one of its branches, like a loop. The loop was hanging four feet off the ground. As I put my arms through the loop and held it underneath my armpits, I was thinking if I let go it would be the end and I would fall off the cliff. I believe in courage because I did it anyway. I know it sounds silly (four feet off the ground) but first I would get a little start by kicking off the ground while someone pushed me. I would swing high in the air around the tree above the cliff. Then I would swing until I stopped with a skid from where I started.

It was amazing, but scary. When someone pushed me I realized I was instantly flying. As I soared over the open space of trees, below me I saw my classmates looking up at me waving. I was so happy that I was screaming with joy. It was so beautiful all the trees and the near by beach. Then, sadly, it was soon over and I stopped from where I started. It was a beautiful experience.

I realized when I was on that swing that courage is a lots of things. Courage is having faith in yourself that you can do anything as long as you try. Courage is facing your fears and being brave. Courage is taking risks and reaching out to accomplish things and to have confidence that you can be successful. Courage is to face difficulty or danger. Courage is having perseverance, saying no the shying away and quitting and to instead think of the things you will do, can do, and will do knowing that if you try you can do many more things in the future. This is why I believe in COURAGE!

I believe in courage because the level of bravery you have doesn't matter until being courageous is the only choice you have. Courage is not doing life threatening stunts to prove yourself, but it is whether you have the perseverance and will-power to finish and fix your actions. Being courageous doesn't have to be a huge, physical thing, but it can be that small action of raising your hand or asking questions when you don't understand. I once had to face a time that may not seem very dramatic to you, but it changed the way I think about courage.

It was late November and my family and I had just moved to the Happy Valley area. By moving here I was about to start the second trimester at Happy Valley Middle School. I was very excited at first because I had many friends there. I couldn't wait for that day to come.

That morning I woke up realizing that today was the day. I was mostly excited about my good friend Maddie showing me around the school. As I was getting ready, a giant knot started to build up in my stomach. I was getting really nervous because I didn't think I was going to be able to start at a new school. All I could think about was how I was going to get through this.

My mom had just packed my lunch and we were ready to go pick up Maddie. On the car ride there I tried taking some deep breathes to calm myself down. We arrived at the school early, so I could meet with the counselor to get my classes. As we walked to each class meeting all the nice teachers, I began feeling a lot more comfortable. At that moment I realized that it was going to be a great year.

During that moment it took a lot of courage to fight my nervousness and start a new school. This wasn't the biggest representation of courage, but it really effected me. It is those little things that make a big difference. Not only in your life, but in the life of others too. This I believe.

I believe if you have courage you can accomplish the impossible. I first learned this when I was 10 years old. I had been doing gymnastics for one year at Sunburst, now Precision Elite. There was one skill I hadn't mastered or done. Giants. Giants aren't the overly tall monsters in fairytales. These giants involve circling a bar with your body relatively straight. Easier said than done.

I was strapped in on the strap bar ready to attempt circling the bar. On the first swing I was anxious to get over but didn't. By the third swing I heard my coach, Denise, yell at me to get over. Doing so, everyone looked over at me and cheered me on. Scared, I closed my eyes and tried my hardest to go over the bar. When I opened them I was on top of the bar. Feeling courageous and ecstatic I did two more, but wanted to stop.

Unknowingly, I bent my arms to try to stop. I remember my friend yelling at me to keep them straight, but I bent them anyway. Therefore, I collapsed on the metal bar. I got off the bar and decided to catch my breath. "Before practice ends you have to do it again," hollered my coach. I nodded that I would. After reassuring myself, I strapped up again. Arguing with myself, I decided to be courageous and try again. "I'm going to do it again," I decided to myself. Going around the bar I did two perfect giants. I successfully accomplished my goal. Feeling pride that I had gone back on the bar and tried again, I left practice with my head held high.

Before I thought that giants were impossible. Now I believe if you have courage, you can accomplish the impossible. "Sometimes even to live is an act of courage."

Courage is a very important value that I strongly believe in. I used to not try anything new. I used to not have any belief in courage. Now I seek opportunities to show and test my courage. The reason I now hold onto this value everywhere I go is all because of one amazing day in the sixth grade.

Our class was on our way to Paradise Trail. Here they had kids test their courage and taught us to trust ourselves. I already had it in my mind that I would not succeed at the part where we climbed a super tall tree and walked on a tightrope to the next tree while reaching for ropes to hold onto for our lives. My mind was full of cowardly ideas of how to get out of it.

Once we got there, my eyes grew huge, and my heart thumped out of my chest. The thing I feared was scarier than I had imagined. Right away kids started up it. Everytime they were done they would say how fun and scary it is. Pretty soon almost everyone had gone, except me.

Just then, as I was sneaking away, my teacher yelled to me that it was my turn. I slowly walked over to her. I told her how I was too afraid and she said, "Breanna, you can do this. I believe in you!" Those words felt wonderful. Then I suddenly realized she was right.

I kicked that fear of heights out of my head, stood up proud, and at that moment I could see courage looking me in the eye. I reached out to it and ever since then I hold onto it everywhere I go.

Middle school, to me, is like a black hole ready to swallow you up. Popular girls act like the fashion police or they diss you because you aren't "cool" enough. A lot of times, girls find themselves in a tricky position. They'll see the most popular girl and try to be like them by changing their clothing style. I myself have attempted this, but soon found that I'm not being true to me. I also found that popular people aren't always the nicest folks walking the halls.

I believe that changing who you are to fit in with the crowd is wrong. People should like you for who you are and <u>not</u> for what you wear. I've noticed a few people I know go "under the spell." It makes me sick to think that one day someone is pretty much a tom-boy, and the next day they're wearing what everyone else is. That's what happened to my best friend. She changed her look and that caused her to become part of the popular group. We aren't friends anymore. She changed who she was to fit in with the crowd. Now, she's fitting in, and I'm at the very bottom of her priority list.

I wish that in middle school everyone treats each other with respect. I wish that there is no such thing as popular, nerd, loser, jock, dweeb, smart, etc. Why don't we all get along? Why does there need to be a social pyramid?

I believe that staying true to yourself and not changing who you are to fit in with the crowd is best for yourself and the other people around you.

Courage

I used to be shy. Now, I am just quiet, that is only if you don't know me. If you knew me, you would know that I am fun, amazing, and sometimes strange and confusing as a jigsaw puzzle. I am like a locked box, for I will only open to those who search for the key. I open up to those who take the time to ask, to wonder if there maybe, just maybe, is something beyond the thin layer of quietness waiting to break.

I had an extreme fear of not being accepted. I was afraid of someone telling me that I was not cool enough or that I did not act the right way, so I just wandered off in my own little world.

Then that day came. I was sitting in the far back of the classroom during story time and I felt someone tap me on the shoulder. I turned my head and furrowed my eyebrows slightly.

"Um," I blinked. "Yes?" I finally managed to whisper. "Well," Daniella, for that was her name, glanced at me, then at the rest of her friends, "we were kind of wondering if you'd want to play with us during recess?" She smiled hopefully, and from that point on, we were best of friends, inseparable.

Those years with her we taught each other so much. She taught me that friendship is a fragile little thing. I taught her it is easily broken. I taught her that it could take you years for you to gain someone's trust. She taught me it takes a minute to lose all. She taught me to apologize. I taught her to forgive.

She did not care how bad I looked or how good I looked. She did not judge me at all for who I was, and now am. Daniela did not give me advice, but offered it. We have a special kind of love, like best friends and sisters put together.

Thinking about this day, which was years ago, I came to the realization of all I had missed out on. Maybe I could have made more friends. It is possible that perhaps the shyness could have only been the cruel effect of having no confidence.   Not to mention every time I see anyone shying away from the rest of the world it infuriates me even more. They just do not know on how much they are missing! They are making the same mistake I made! Oh and I know for sure that they are going to look back, years after—much like the way I did—and think that they could have done more, they could have done better.

I believe that confidence is not letting your fears take the lead. Do what you are destined to do with pride and with your head held high. I believe in being yourself and accepting others for who they are because life is not about loving a perfect person, but about loving an imperfect person perfectly, a best friend or someone far beyond that, this I believe.

I believe that no matter how hard something is, you can do it with some confidence. Just like when I was doing my state writing test. It happened when I was 12 years old and I was in 7th grade. It happened in my classroom, room number 302. Mr. Boyd, our principal, was the one who was involved. So, I was writing my state writing, and I wasn't very confident. This is the pre, kind of, and I guess it's like a practice. I was writing and when it was time to hand over the practice writing, I was already done, but I still wasn't very confident. After they graded my writing, we all got ours back. I looked at my grades while the other people looked at theirs. I got almost all 4's except for two scores. The two scores were under 4 and I felt pretty unconfident about the subjects that got marked down. After a day or so, we had to have a meeting with either my teacher, our principal, our vice principal, or a lady. I had to meet with our principal. When the person in front of me was done with their meeting, it was time for me to go and have a conference. I told him I wasn't very confident about my writing. So he told me that I should think more positively and get more confidence about my writing. After that meeting, I am always more confident about my writing when I do write. That is why I believe that no matter how hard something is, you can do it with some confidence. This I believe!

I believe in confidence because having the strength and courage to do something can be very successful in life.

Confidence is believing in yourself and having the courage to stand up for what you believe in. Having confidence in yourself is a key to being successful. Being confident doesn't have to be a huge stunt, but it can be that small action when rising above and being strong.

It was the summer time in Happy Valley, Oregon. Middle school was starting up and everyone was going to register for the year. Children were anxious to get their locker combination and see all their friends again. On the other hand, my friend Kelsie and I were nervous to jump up to middle school and start at a brand new big school with both seventh and eighth graders. Getting to go to six different classes and only four minutes to transfer to your next class can get stressful. In addition, coming home at four o'clock with lots of homework can be hard, too.

The first day was going to take a lot of confidence and bravery. I was getting ready in my bathroom, doing my hair, making sure I looked great for the first day. While brushing my teeth, all of the sudden I start feeling butterflies flying around in my stomach going crazy. I go so nervous I was scared to get out of the car. When I got to school and saw all my friends with big bright smiles looking excited, the butterflies seemed to calm down more. I walked into the gym to receive my schedule and compared them with friends. I was so relieved. Jade, one of my good friends, had all of the same classes as me. My best friend, Kelsie, also had three of our core classes together. My butterflies disappeared and I was perfectly fine the rest of the day.

At the end of the day, I realized that I can believe in myself to have the confidence to start middle school with everyone else at a new school. I was confident, and this I believe.

I believe each individual possesses a unique set of special talents, interests, and strengths. Middle school is the perfect time to explore, find out what you're good at, what you enjoy, and most importantly what makes you who you are.

During your middle school years you may discover that you love science, are a talented musician in the band, and a loyal friend. Or, you may find that you love to write, are a star at cross country meets, and your neighbors seem to always call on you to babysit because you're great with little kids. Make sure to experience and explore a wide range of activities and topics so that you don't miss out on something you were meant to enjoy. Don't be afraid to try new things either. Learning that you don't really excel at basketball or playing the piano is an important part of your journey. You'll never know until you try.

When you begin to discover what it is that you're good at, what you enjoy, what your interests are, it is important to develop and nurture those gifts. If you find you're passionate about history, keep taking classes and reading books. If you discover you're skillful at speaking in front of others, put even more effort into that next class speech or consider running for student council. Some individuals are blessed with the ability to help others. If this is you, keep helping and reaching out to those who need you.

Middle school is an exciting, crazy and sometimes awkward time of your life. You're growing, changing and finding out who you are. So keep an open mind, try new things, and seek to find your special talents, interests and strengths. Be the best YOU that you can be! This I believe.

-Staff

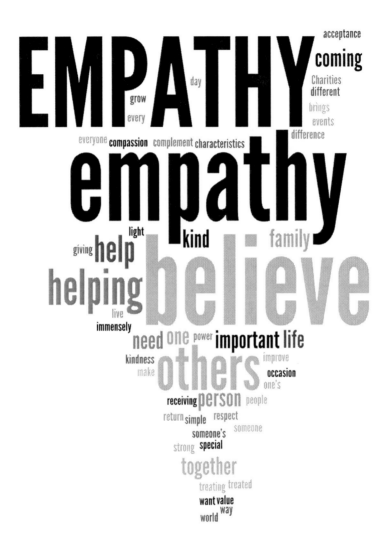

By helping others grow, you are helping yourself. Charities are events at which you can help people in need. You can help others in need by donating money, time, or even positive thoughts for them. Helping at charities is an easy way to show empathy towards others. It is also away of showing hope that these people can dust themselves off and stand up to live a happy life.

Every December, there is an event called Winter Rage that is hosted by Clackamas High School. Winter Rage is an event where the people that live in the Clackamas-Happy Valley area help others who are in need. This is done by donating clothes, shoes, household supplies, non-perishable foods, or even money. Each year students, teachers, and parents come to the school to organize donated items, wrap presents for kids in need, and pack food boxes. Some of the older students take their cars to go collect items from around the Clackamas-Happy Valley areas. This has been a successful charity for 13 years. In addition to all those items donated the school then donates the excess items to larger charities in the Portland areas.

Just last December was a Winter Rage that helped 265 families in needs and it was a great success. There were piles of clothes, canned foods, toys, and loads of people helping, including my family. Every year my family devotes our whole day to help out at the school. We fold clothes, organize food boxes, and even wrap presents for the little kids. The week before Winter Rage we go shopping for presents for the kids of the families in need. Just helping these people bring joy to my family. During the Christmas season the greatest gift I received was the gift of giving.

After the organizing is finished, the families in need come to pick up their "presents". Showing these people around is such a joy because the greatest thing to see is their face light up with happiness. When I see these people I feels as if they are my own family. It feels as if helping them is the right thing to do and it is. That was the day I felt true joy in my life. Now, I understand that helping others is helping you.

Before this, I felt selfish and didn't feel like helping others. I didn't feel like helping others. I didn't know the joy of helping others. Now, I know the joy of receiving the gift of giving. I also know that charity is something you can do to help the world. Prior to Winter Rage I didn't know this was an important value until I experienced it. Realizing that many people around me need help was the number one thing I learned. I believe in the power of charity because helping others is helping you.

Personally, I don't believe in the way our species is going. I've almost given up on our survival. Through all of the negativity and frustration in my life and the lives of everyone else on this planet I still have one belief that stands strong. I believe that others come before you. Lately, however I have observed that people don't follow this important rule, people will go through life caring about nobody but themselves, and where do those people get? Nowhere, absolutely nowhere. About a year ago I discovered this. I used to care about nobody but myself. Life was all about me and whether or not I was successful. If others had to be hurt along the way, so be it. The only life that mattered was mine. As I was going through this process, I felt terrible. I felt depressed, frustrated, jealous, regretful, and negative--emotions you can come up with, I felt all at once. Although the thing that truly amazed me was that people put their problems aside so they could help me through mine. I would think to myself, "Why are they doing this?" It is because if you help people, they in return will help you. When one person does something good it inspires others to do so as well. Then the cycle begins. People doing one good thing will lead to another good thing which of course would lead to another good thing. Then after a while we would have everyone in the world putting others before themselves and lending a hand when they need to. With a world like this there would be no war, very little hunger, and very little poverty. Our world would be near perfect and anyone would live the life they wanted to. So what do I believe? I believe in the power of kindness, respect, empathy, and helping someone who is in need.

Empathy

I believe that compassion brings some light to an ever-dark world. I believe this because one day on winter break this year, I bought, made and delivered five homemade blankets to the homeless people of downtown Portland. I bought the material, my Grandma made them, and my dad helped me deliver the blankets. When I look back on that day, I remember feeling chilled and nervous, but when I saw their smiles and their thankfulness, I warmed up on the inside and I wasn't as nervous as I had been.

Before this experience, I thought that homeless people were just like the hobos everyone said they were, but now I know that they are different, but exactly like us in more ways than one. I used to value that I should help when I can, but otherwise let nature take its course. Now I value that we should help people whenever you can, as much as possible.

This is why I believe compassion brings some light to a some times dark world.

I believe in empathy and acceptance. I have believed both of these arts/feelings since I was eight years old. It happened at a park in Shingle Springs, California. I was swinging on the swings with my friend; we were watching the new kid. He looked over at us from the side; we giggled and blushed. We had no idea at the time that he was lonely or scared—all we knew was that he was cute. We saw him at school the next day. He sat alone and in the back of the classroom. The school day went by slowly. When the bell rang for recess, all the kids, including my friends and I, ran outside to play. Well, almost all the kids. He walked out slowly and cautiously. Then, about halfway through recess, he got up to play basketball with some of the other kids. As the new kid walked up to the courts, the other kids stopped playing and watched him. He stopped, unsure of whether to continue or not. One particularly large boy approached him and told him he couldn't play and shoved the new kid backwards. He fell. By now everyone was watching—especially me, and I had had enough and so had my friends. We walked over to the new kid and I asked him if he wanted to play on the playground with us. He looked scared, but he agreed anyways. We spent the rest of recess laughing and having fun. Even today we are still friends.

I believe in empathy and acceptance and that when it comes down to it, those are two pretty good traits to have and use. This I believe.

Something I value and believe in is empathy. Empathy means to understand another person's feelings, situations, and motives. I started understanding empathy in 7th grade when my friend was talking to me about her problem with her family.

It was in 7th grade in the girls' bathroom at Sunrise Middle School. It was just her and I. The bathroom was really small, bright and pretty empty except for me and her. It wasn't the cleanest place in the school, but it was a pretty good place to talk.

At the time, I remember feeling so happy and proud that she was able to talk to me about her problems and I still feel the same way today. At first, I really didn't think putting yourself in people's shoes and understanding what people go through was that big of a deal, but now I know it's a huge deal because it makes it way more easy for people to talk to you about their problems. At first I thought honesty and friendship were the most important things to have but now I can add empathy to that list.

Right now, a few things I value or believe in are honesty, trust, friendship, getting good grades and of course, empathy.

    I believe in strong empathy with others and coming together as a family. Over winter break my brother went through major reconstruction surgery. He would have been home for Christmas, but something went wrong during his recovery. This tragic event had him back in the hospital on Christmas day. My brother and I were home alone for most of the day. When he and I awoke on Christmas, we didn't go downstairs as a whole family to open presets like we do every year. I was very empathetic for my brother being in the hospital because I, too, once was in a hospital on a vacation. I was really sick when my family and I went to Canada. Since I was terribly sick, we basically had to stop the whole vacation and end it early. This helped me relate to my brother when he was in the hospital because we both knew what it was like to end a vacation for the entire family.

    From this major event it helped me realize that I have been taking Christmas for granted. I thought it was about tradition, but now I know it is about being with my family. This realization has made me a stronger person when it comes to celebrating holidays. You never realize how good something is until it is gone and you are left alone. I can now even share my empathy towards my brother being in the hospital. This I believe: in empathy and coming together as a family on a special occasion.

    I believe that empathy can make all the difference in someone's life. The night that my grandma died, I cried and cried. I thought that nothing could heal the big hole in my heart. When I came to school the next day, empty and beaten down, no one could cheer me up with a smile or a laugh. I stumbled into choir and all I could think about was my grandma, but my friends came to my aid—especially one friend in particular. When I told her that my grandma had passed away, she knew exactly how I felt because the same thing had happened to her. We talked and she told me how she had felt when her grandpa had passed; then she told me that no matter what, she would always be there for me. I know anyone of my other friends could have told me the same thing, but when someone knows, and can relate to your situation, it has so much more meaning. I learned the effects of empathy that day and I will never forget them because not only can empathy change someone's life, it changed mine.

I believe in empathy, and treating others the way you want to be treated yourself. I believe in respect, and integrity and dignity. I believe in good character. When I was in 5th grade at Spring Mt. Elementary, I wasn't exactly the most popular kid--in fact people called me fat and nerdy. One incident that is still with me and inspires me to help out other kids that aren't too "cool" is the day I got my cell phone. I was so happy. I thought life couldn't get any better. All the kids wanted to see it and hold it, and a girl in particular told me they were allowed in school. This happened to be the girl I had a crush on. Stupidly, I pulled it out and showed it to her in the middle of class. The teacher saw it and took it. I started crying, the whole class was laughing and I felt like the dumbest kid in the world. I went to the bathroom, where I sobbed like a two year old…until something strange, unusual, and incredible happened that I still remember to this day. The "coolest" kid in the school, the most popular kid that everyone followed, came into the bathroom. I stood there, thinking he was going to make fun of me. But he said, "Hey, it's okay. Sorry everyone laughed—that was rude." He gave me a pat on the back and said, "I got you your phone back from the teacher. It's recess now. Come play basketball with us?"

"Sure," I said. And that random act of kindness made my day. I learned that one random act of kindness can turn someone's whole day around for the better. I believe in empathy. I believe in respect, and I believe in random acts of kindness. "You never know when you have the chance to change someone's life."

I believe in empathy, because everyone is different. It all started when I first came to Kindergarten and I didn't really know English. It was really hard for me to understand people and it was really hard for people to understand me. There were different languages all over the class. But, for me it seemed like I was the only one who didn't understand anyone and anything. It took a lot of hard work for teachers to help me. In about four weeks I slowly began to speak English.

I believe in empathy because it really helped me. If everyone had empathy, the world would be a much better place. Schools would be better and teachers would be better.

    I believe that empathy is one of the most important characteristics to have. This trait is important to have because it helps you understand what people are going through. This allows you to be able to help them in their particular situation, because you yourself know what it was like to go through.

    It was a warm spring day. Every bird was chirping, every blade of grass was swaying with the soft breeze, and every boy was outside playing football. My friends and I were at the park playing a game of pick-up football. Everything was perfect, until a nerdy looking kid from school cautiously walked over to us. He introduced himself and very hesitantly asked if he may join in. My friends looked him up and down and decided he was no athlete. Cameron, one of my friends, said that maybe he could play another time. Cameron couldn't do it with a straight face. Lucas, the shy nerd looked like a spear had just pierced him. He did his best to hide his emotions. His best wasn't very good. He walked away after a shaky "oh, ok." We went right back to playing once he left.

    The next day was even better than the first. After I had a snack I noticed some older kids playing football at the park. I quickly ran over and asked if I could play. The kids said "yeah, right," and went right back to playing. This absolutely crushed me. I was completely hurt, but I hid my feelings from the group. I walked back to my house at a turtle rate, thinking about why I couldn't play, and what was wrong with me.

Empathy

A week later my friends and I were playing basketball outside. We saw Luke come over again with much hesitance. Once again he asked if he could join in. The second he asked that, a bunch of emotions slapped me across the face: pain, humiliation and despair. I realized that these emotions were the feelings I felt when I was turned down, and the emotions Luke must have felt last time we denied him. I could see that Brandon was about to shoot him down again. I quickly said "sure!" Everyone looked at me like what the heck are you doing? I told them to just let him play. Once we got the game started it turned out that Luke was actually a pretty good player. We played until the night sky turned orange.

It turned out that Luke was a very good player that day. It also felt good that I let Luke play and stopped him from feeling the horrible emotions I felt when I was rejected. It was all because I knew how he felt. That is why I believe that empathy is one of the most important characteristics.

I believe in empathy because of something that happened in fifth grade.

It was a sunny day, with a bit of wind and the trees had beautiful leaves. The day was amazing for all the kids at Mt. Scott except for one girl who sat alone on a loud bus crying.

I knew how she felt. Sometimes I just want to cry. When I feel like that, what I really want is for someone to comfort me. The very next thing I thought was that I should be that person, the one to comfort and help when no one else will. So I did.

Just before the bus started I stood up and walked slowly to her seat. She looked at me with watery eyes. Then I asked her what was wrong and she told me. I listened quietly untill she was finished. I gave her some good advice and she smiled graciously as I got off the bus. I went home that day feeling good about myself and great that I could help someone that needed it.

I believe in empathy because of this experience. I now know that now I just feel sad sometimes.

This I believe; a simple complement can improve one's day immensely. It was a Monday. It's a usual Monday where you're tired, bored and hungry no matter what. And to add to the Monday morning madness, I was having a bad day. Nothing seemed to be going right for me, and every playful putdown was a dagger through my stomach.

I was sitting at my desk in class writing a paper, when I heard some one behind me tell me they like my haircut. I half turned in my chair and murmured, "Thanks." A few moments later-in a mocking tone-came a; "Yeah! Love your hair!" Apparently they'd overheard the complement I'd received. I sighed and rolled my eyes. "No, really, it's cool…" They continued, their voice evening out to a normal tone, now. "I was a bit in awe from this unexpected remark, and managed a mere, "Thanks." Needless to say as I walked out of that class, my heart was racing a little faster and my metaphorical smile was a lot larger.

The simple power of a complement is larger than life. There really doesn't seem to be a way to receive a sincere complement and not let it even fazes you.

Now, I realize that whether someone says they like your haircut, your outfit, or your social studies project, you should always take it to heart. Let it break the metaphorical clouds of your day, so you can pass on that light.

    I learned that although my father, mother, brother, grandparents and husband have passed away, I believe that life's struggles teach you compassion, empathy, hope and interdependence for one another. I learned this over my lifetime, but especially the last six years.

    During that time both my husband and I had some very serious and life threatening health issues. I learned that even in the darkest times, how you treat others and how they treat you is so important. My husband and I were very supportive of each other and because each of us were having these issues we were able to give comfort to each other. We learned patience for each other and if we were grumpy because we didn't feel well, we just sluffed it off and accepted that we were having a bad day.

    Another thing I learned was to trust in the Lord. He made my days and nights much more manageable, because He is always with me. If my day was difficult to handle all I had to do was call on Him. He provided peace when things were grim. I learned that no matter how many people you lose in your lifetime that if you're determined then you can go forward with your life and gain great strength of character. It isn't easy to lose loved ones, but you can over come the losses by doing what is right and hoping that you would make the person proud if they were still with you.

    I learned that although my father, mother, brother, grandparents and husband had all passed away that each of them loved me and had a good influence on my life. I also know that each one of them is still with me and few days go by that I don't think about them. I am encouraged by having had them, even though it was only for a short time.

This I believe.

-Staff

I believe that it's always possible to find empathy for those close and far. Recently my father came to stay with my family for one whole month. He was going to fly to Portland from Texas and live in my house for one whole month. I thought he was joking when I read his e-mail.

My parents divorced in 1978, that's just two years after "me". My sister and I would visit him in the summers when we were younger (I still can't stand the Texas heat) but eventually as we found ourselves summer jobs the visits faded away. I never understood why they divorced and why my dad would move so far away from his family. I grew up not understanding where he really came from and this turned into bitterness towards my father. When we would communicate it would be about the greatness of Ted Williams or about how he thought the Red Sox could finally win the World Series. I always treasured these conversations with him, but they just left me upset that we couldn't have any real father-son conversations.

I've been blessed with two sons of my own and now my father wanted to fly in to spend some quality time with his two grandsons. When he arrived he shared with me that he was writing a play based on journals that his grandfather gave him and as part of the production he would include what little photos he had of growing up in Boston. He wanted me to help revise his play and he also wanted to explain some of his family photos.

My father's story was about growing up as a deaf child in a hearing world. His mother abandoned four children and left them with an alcoholic father. He was split from his siblings and raised by his grandfather. He found it strange that his grandfather gave him his journals since he never really "communicated" with him. He then told me that he understood we also never "communicated" or had deep conversations while I was growing up. This was my father's way of trying to explain things from his perspective.

Through his play and photos we spent the whole month learning about his life while he met mine. I finally understood where he was from. My two sons loved when he would read them stories. I recalled the stories he would entertain my sister and I with on our early visits. Thought of the good times we did share together and of a future with a father who has also become a grandfather. Now that I understand some of his life experiences I have become a better person. I believe that it's always possible to find empathy for those close and far.

-Staff

    I believe that you can always trust and get help from friends. I moved to America three years ago in the 4th grade. When I came, I wasn't prepared for anything because at the time I couldn't speak English or even understand. I was worried that I would never fit in and that no one will like me.

    The first person that really helped me was Micah. She told me everything I needed to know and also introduced me to her friends. The first day of school when Micah talked to me, I was surprised that someone was willing to talk to me and didn't seem to be nervous at all. Even though I couldn't quite understand, when Micah started talking to me, I knew we were going to be friends.

    As days passed, I started getting used to everything and everyone around me. I had hope again that I could fit in and not be someone who sat alone at the lunch table. I was proud that I made friends and was happy that I was not someone who everybody hates.

    Now, the most important things that I value are friendship, trust and love. Trust can lead up to making good friends, and friends lead to love. If I hadn't made friends in 4th grade, I wouldn't be the person I am now. I hope that I can keep my amazing friends forever. My friends are the most important people in the world for me.

I believe in forgiveness because everyone should get a second chance. I didn't give my friend a second chance and now we aren't friends anymore. That's why forgiveness is important.

My friend and I played basketball almost every day. Then we would go over to either my house or his. We would play GameCube or Playstation 2. Sometimes we would watch a movie, but not very often. When we got bored of basketball we would play football or baseball. It was the best.

In the summer we would ride our bikes over to the park. On the Fourth of July we would go over to the park and ride the mechanical bull. We would always think of something fun to do.

One day we were playing basketball and I was beating him and he got really mad. He threw my basketball on the ground and popped it. He ran into his house and left me speechless. It made me really mad. The next day, when he came over and didn't apologize, I told him to get out.

I believe in forgiveness because everyone deserves a second chance. I didn't give him a second chance and now we aren't friends. Everyone deserves second chances.

I believe in friendship because friends help each other through the ups and downs. It was the weekend before my friend, Vicky's birthday. She only invited me and our friend, Teresa. When I got there, I saw that Vicky's baby brother had broken his arm! He was wearing a Charlie Brown cast. He's so cute! Then, he and his sister Kaylee came up and hugged me. I said hi to everyone and, Vicky, Kaylee, and I went to Vicky's room. We started to paint Kaylee's toes. Vicky and I failed at it. We finally got it to perfection and her toes were an aqua blue.

Later on, Teresa came. We started to tell secrets. Then we talked about relationship problems. When I was sad they were there for me. So, I was also there for them. We were out of problems and went downstairs to watch a movie. It was 12 am. We grabbed a carton of ice cream and all started eating out of it. We always have a lot of fun when we're together. But, the sad part is that we all go to different schools. Teresa goes to Benson High, Vicky goes to Bismead Middle, Kaylee is four, and I go to Happy Valley Middle School. We had a lot of fun. I believe in friendship.

Trust is earned slowly, but lost quickly! But for me it was the opposite!

About 5 or 6 years ago, one of the many scary things in my life happened! I was climbing a really old big tree and I was almost to the top of the tree when all-of-a-sudden a wasp stung my head.

Next thing I know was that I was falling. I fell 50 or 60 feet to the ground. Hitting branches and twigs (slowing me down).

Now before I tell the rest of my story I want you to know my older brother is mean, big, strong, and mean! So of course I didn't trust him, not one bit (I'm exaggerating).

When I finally hit the ground I realized I had an inch deep gash on my stomach (not my belly button) an inch wide, deep and blood, gash on my stomach.

I thought I was going to die right then and there! Until I felt like I was being lifted up and moving towards my house at 100 mph. (I was 8 so it felt fast) It was my older brother, he was so fast… and he was crying? That's one of the most vivid memories of that time.

I turned out ok and got a few punches from my brother (calling me stupid). The rest of the time was spent listening to him trying to explain why he was crying (saying a wasp stung him). I think he was really crying because he cared about me.

Trust can come in many different forms. Take me for example, I now trust my older brother (because he

116   *Friendship*

saved my life and stands up for me [even if I'm wrong]) I believe that you can trust anyone you know.

This I believe. I believe in forgiveness. The reason I believe in forgiveness is because it would be world wars but forever. I would have no friends. All friends have ups and downs and they all need to forgive each other at one point to stay friends.

Another thing I believe is not to criticize people from their looks. You always hear kids say, "Oh, he must be a pothead," or some other stereotype when the person could have been a bad hair day. I mean come on, give someone a break . A lot of immature kids see someone once and stamp them for life. Talk to them before you decide.

The third thing I believe in is a good word choice. You don't need to use verbal abuse or cussing to prove a point. For example, "you dumb ***," the better choice is, "that wasn't very smart of you." It just isn't needed in your life everyday. Its pointless.

This leads to a fourth thing I believe in not doing, it is talking behind someone's back. If you have something to say then please step up, if your too much of a coward to say it to their face don't say it at all.

That is some of the things I believe in and use in my everyday life, and you should too!

Sometimes the best times in your life are spent with just you and your best friends. I believe in friendship.

We just finished our homework and we decided to play with this inflatable globe ball. We were playing volleyball until the ball went over the couch! "I'll get it!" I said as I was walking toward the couch. "No!! You're supposed to do it like this!" my friend Lizzy said as she jumped over the couch and as she was sliding down it like a penguin on its belly sliding on ice, her foot went up and she accidentally kicked me right in the thigh! I let out a frilly scream and all of a sudden we started cracking up! But this wasn't an ordinary silly moment with your best friend, we were laughing and literally ROFLing! (Rolling On the Floor Laughing) for all you non-texting folks out there.

After laughing for about a good 5 minutes, we stood up. "We need a name for this moment." I said while wiping away the tears. "How about global... something with global." "Global Warning!! We said together. And let me just tell you, that memory will always remind me that without friendship, there isn't humor. And without humor, then what kind of life are you living girl!!

Live and prosper everyday of your life. Because you don't know what you've got, until it's gone. ☺

Friendship

I believe that forgiveness is the answer to all problems. It was a sunny day and my friend Dylan called over to see if I wanted to hang out so I went over to his house. We started to play football when we got to his backyard. Then Dylan stopped and said I was a cheater and I was a sore loser. Dylan got up and ran to his swing mad and I got going to walk home because I was upset and wanted to go home.

As I walked by Dylan he pushed me to the ground now I was mad and I went and pushed him back but then he came and kicked me as hard as he could and I flew back my body was sore so then I yelled forget you. After that day we didn't talk for weeks finally he called me he asked if I could come over so he could tell me something.

When I got to his house I asked what he wanted. Dylan said that he was sorry for everything he said to me ditto me and I said was sorry too. We said we would never call each other a cheater, liar, or dumb. Now Dylan and me are best friends and we hang out with each other mostly every day. Forgiveness made it so that me and Dylan are best friends.

    I believe that friendship helps people live a happy life. From second to fifth grade I lived in Kansas, and on my very first day I had made a forever friend. Her name was Ashley, we sat right next to each other and started talking. We found that we had a lot of things in common such as…we both liked cheese, pink, gymnastics, etc. So from now to back then we have been friends.

    Two years later we were in the 4th grade where we could not stop talking. We got in trouble and it was the best year of school. In social studies the class split up into two groups (ones that understood and one that didn't) Ashley and I always knew what we were doing. So because we did we went to the corner of the class and read the chapter in the book, then talk while answering the questions. We called this "social" study. Later that year was her birthday so we went to the movies, swimming at the indoor water park, and getting pizza. We stayed up really late watching movies and talking.

    One of the last memories I have with her is before I moved, she invited a bunch of our friends over to throw me a surprise going away party. We all went swimming in her pool, ate pizza, and had fun.

    Those four years were some of the best in my life. From the start I made wonderful friends. I believe that friendship helps people live a happy life.

Friendship

I believe in trust, because a couple of years ago in the summer I was hanging out with my cousin. We both were riding bikes, and I knew there was something wrong about the bike I was riding. So I took a risk and kept on riding it. Suddenly I was going really fast on my bike until I heard the chain break and I fell face first on the concrete, then the bike fell on top of me. My legs got stuck on the bike and I couldn't take them out. When my cousin heard the crash, he came out as fast as he can. When he came, he got the bike out of my legs and told his brother to take the bike back to the house, and he would help me get back to the house to relax. When we got back to his house, I was bleeding on my legs, my arms and my face. After I stopped bleeding my grandma called my relative to come and fix the bike. When he came he didn't fix the bike, he taught me how to fix the bike. He told me if it ever happens again then I would know what to do. So I learned to trust my cousin more often, and if it wasn't for him helping me, I would have scars on my legs.

I believe in loyalty because without loyalty people would never see things through until the end. Loyalty is important in every job that people have to do, an engineer can't cancel a contract because he doesn't like the tools he is given. Up until recently I didn't know a lot about loyalty. I was, and still am, a quiet kid who got good grades. The people I have remained most loyal to are my family.

On December 22nd over winter break I was just sitting around in my basement late at night watching t.v. My dad had been getting into a lot of arguments with my aunt. It was getting late so I went out into the garage to check on my dad. When I got out to the garage he fell over onto a pile of boxes and blankets and so I helped him up. I could barely hold a coherent conversation, he was very, very tired and I helped him into the house. After that I had to let him sit down because I was having trouble holding him up. We sat for a few minutes talking, then I helped him up and we started up for the stairs. The stairs were the hardest part because I was supporting a lot of weight and his feet kept falling out from under him. When we finally got to my parents room I was tired but I helped him sit down and take off his shoes and socks off. Then my mom woke up and I had to leave. My theory was proved when he slept to almost noon. I believe in loyalty because without it I would not had the courage to help my dad. The beliefs I now hold close are: loyalty, integrity, and courage because without those things we wouldn't have the world we have today.

Friendship

This I believe: Trust is the most important thing someone could have. This is because without trust, you wouldn't be able to have true friends. You have to trust someone to be friends with them. I learned the value of trust at my daycare 4 years ago. My friend and I were sitting at one of the lunch tables talking. All of the sudden a bigger kid ran over and pushed my friend to the ground. He backed up and stood there. I jumped up and told him to stop. My friend trusted me in the way that I wouldn't leave him on the ground. The big kid wanted to hurt him. My friend was smaller than me and the big boy was bigger than both of us. I told the boy he would regret doing this. Out of nowhere, he threw scissors at my face. One missed, but one hit me right on the side of my left eye. It broke the skin and was bleeding everywhere. The boy ran and I tackled him. The teacher ran over to stop us. We both got in trouble, but once the teacher saw the gash on my face, the boy didn't come to daycare for awhile. My friend who watched all of this from the ground was amazed. He trusted me. He knew I wasn't going to leave him. Me and him are still good friends. If you trust your friends, they will trust you. Also, you and that person are going to be friends a long time.

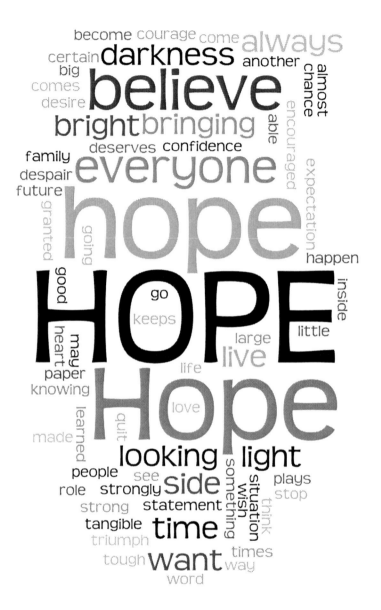

    I believe that there is good in everyone. I believe everyone deserves a chance. The summer of fifth grade was the year I would start over and be who I wanted to be. I still remember the day my mom came home and decided to surprise my sister and I by telling us we were moving the minute my sister finished painting her room. My face fell into despair and my sister just looked at her in silence. The next couple of weeks we were hard at work with trying to throw out all of the junk in our house we had kept for years and collected plenty of dust. In just a couple of months we had moved to a new house in the quaint suburbs of Happy Valley. It was the middle of July when we had started to settle into our new life.

    It was the day before school started and I couldn't sleep. It was nerve-racking because I never had gone to any other school and I would be made to start all over and wouldn't have anyone to talk to. The next morning I rolled out of bed and got ready for my new school. My head spun as I got out of the car that morning as I walked through the front door and watched kindergartners scramble through the crowd. They examined the school in awe as their parents staggered behind them holding all of their school supplies. All of a sudden, I heard a loud whoop from behind me. He stumbled into me as kids pushed past him. He smiled and went with the flow of the kids around him. I went downstairs and stepped into my new home for the next year. I stood in the doorway as I saw a class full of wild 5th graders chasing each other around the room. A boy named Eric spotted me from across the room and swirled around the desk. He greeted me and asked about me. Eric showed me around and introduced me to his friend Alex. When he approached me, I noticed it was the same boy I had ran into earlier. He was really nice and invited me to hang out with him at recess. As the bell rang I sat down at an empty desk ready for my first day.

The class played lots of games that included having to remember everyone's name and a partner game. That's when I met my best friend in elementary school. Her name was Laura and was also new to the area. For the last two years of my elementary school career I met lots of new friends along the way. The experience of moving to a new school showed me that everyone is very friendly to you and really try to get to know you and also makes you feel comfortable in the new community for you. This whole experience though, shows acceptance because everyone accepted me for who I was even if they really did not know me. I believe that if you give everyone a chance, they will accept you no matter what happens. This I believe.

    I believe in hope, and I believe that if everyone has the will to live, they can live. My dad didn't have the will to live and he almost didn't make it through his surgeries.

    During the summer of the 7th grade, my dad found out he had a tumor in his colon. His surgery was scheduled for a month later, and a stressful surgery it was. As he was in surgery, I sat in a huge waiting room filled with windows, maroon couches, and a snack bar. Sitting in there was the hardest thing I've ever had to do. Not knowing my dad's condition was nerve-racking. After three hours, the doctor came and told us my dad was all right, and we could see him soon.

    When we finally got to go into his room, he looked very different. He had swollen up two times his regular size, but only his stomach. The doctors had not stitched him up all the way and it allowed poisons to enter his stomach. He could barely move, and barely breathe. I remember exactly what he said to me that moment as I walked in, "Honey, even if I don't make it, always remember I love you no matter what." After that the nurse rolled him out the door and to emergency surgery.

    All I remember thinking was that I had to stay strong and hope that God would let a miracle happen. Then when I turned my head I saw my mom crying while talking to my aunt. My dad did live, but I will never forget that hope and his will to live, for me, was what kept him alive.

I have learned to go for what I want and believe in. I have grown up with a wonderful life, and being surrounded by friends and family. My grandparents, parents, and sister were so supportive of me and helpful, so when it came to 6th grade when my grandfather died, it took my whole family and I by surprise. No one knew it was coming and we were all devastated. It was like most of the glue keeping our family together had just come undone. I felt like if I would have spent more time with him I would have changed what happened. I could have helped, but I felt like a helpless little kid who couldn't do anything to help in the family situation. I was like a spectator on a side line instead of being in the game.

After this event, it made me think of other things other than my own problems; it made me think of the amazing things that my grandfather did to help people and the community. Seeing and listening to people go on and on about how great he was, made me realize what I can do to help and be known as a great person too. Even though he was gone and out of our lives in one way, he was still helping us get through the hard times. He was a great man and I really hope that some day I can be like him.

I believe that hope is a little word on paper, but it is a big statement in my heart. Hope keeps you going when you want to stop and quit. If my family didn't have hope, love, or didn't believe, we wouldn't have become strong and knowing that we made it through a tough time and that we can do it again if another situation comes our way. Because of hope, I feel like I can do anything and be so much help and be a great leader just like my grandfather. I know if I give up and don't have hope and believe I shut down and don't get anywhere. But I know if I have hope in my heart and mind the sky is the limit for me and I can accomplish anything in life. I can be a leader and be known for doing something great, if I believe in myself. I believe in hope.

I believe hope can triumph in times of despair. When we flew home for Christmas last year, I knew there was something wrong. My Dad had been to the doctor. He's never had a stitch, a broken bone, or so much as a cavity. "He never goes to the doctor," I thought.

After Christmas dinner, when our whole family was at the table, my Dad gave us the news: he had cancer. Each of us was stunned and, in our own ways, we all began to cope with cancer.

My father's colon was removed early one winter morning. We expected it to be partially removed, but the cancer was invasive.

Another surgery followed and another one after that. Throughout that long winter, my family burned up the phone lines, sharing the details of my Dad's illness, practicing for when things would get worse, but always looking for signs of hope. "He's lost 50 lbs.," said my brother, "but he has good color in his face. And he laughed a little today."

Every day I talked to someone in my family and I clung to their hopeful words and stories. Every conversation ended with, "He's going to make it," and "I love you." It was so important to keep saying those things, to keep reminding each other that there was hope and that we as a family, had what we needed to save Dad's life.

After four surgeries and five months of hospitals and doctors, my Dad is free of cancer, healthy, happy and strong. Even though it was the darkest winter, I never gave up hope that spring would come and that he would make it.

Hope triumphs over despair. This I believe.

Hope is something I believe in so strongly that to me, hope is almost tangible. I may not be able to see it, but it is always with me. Hope plays a large role in my life and I think about it all the time.

The day the high school counselor came to my school and talked to the class about high school forecasting, was the day when hope showed up and surprised me. As I looked through all of the information about Clackamas High School, I realized that I had an incredible amount of hope and options for my future. I realized that I have hope for a very bright future. I have hope for becoming whatever I want to be. I have hope of making a difference in the world. Even as I write this, I feel the overwhelming feeling of hope and what I am capable of.

I found hope in a very unexpected place. When I wasn't searching for it, hope found me. It may seem like such an insignificant thing, but this event showed me a whole new side of hope that I had never seen. This is why I believe in hope.

I believe in hope. Hope doesn't always come from the inside, it can be encouraged by other people.

With only two laps left I started to lose hope that I could keep my place to the finish. This was only my first middle school track meet, and I wanted to keep up with my teammate who was running almost side-by-side with me. Breathing really hard, feeling pain in my legs, I tried to keep up with her. Right before I was about to slow down she asked me if I was okay. Answering in between breaths I told her that I was getting really tired. Encouraging statements like "you can do it", "you're doing great" and "we're almost done" came from her. The next thing I knew I had hope again.

That simple phrase made me believe that I could finish my race strong. The rest of the race went by quickly. Running through my head were the words said by my teammate. When I crossed the finish, I was relieved that the hope from her lasted the whole way. Not only did I finish, but I got a personal record. I believe in hope.

In the year 2004, my mom went into the hospital looking like she was seven months pregnant. She was very sick and couldn't eat anything. I was scared and confused. A week after testing my mom for all of these different problems that could be occurring the doctors found out her large colon didn't work anymore so the doctors would have to take it out. With my mom not working and my dad on a low income, we had no money for the surgery. My grandparents ended up paying for it because my dad couldn't.

As my mom went under, we all said goodbye and slowly walked into the waiting room where all we had with us was hope that she would make it. We sat in that gross waiting room for what felt like forever.

After the surgery they wouldn't let us see her because she was still asleep. All we had was hope, and it worked because my mom is still alive today. Even though she can no longer work. I believed in hope and hope heard me and healed my mom to the point where she and I run marathons together.

My belief is hope. A great experience at that moment I was in. I was twelve at that time. I was doing bad in school but one thing I cherished was my music. See, I was a guitarist in my band and vocals #2. We always tried to get into a gig. We wrote many songs and always enjoyed ourselves. The story started when we were trying to get ourselves in something called light café. We've been trying to get in it for months! Light café was on the last Friday of every month but we kept getting rejected. I knew we could do it so I never gave up. They finally accepted us and I knew that hope was always on my side. I will never forget that moment. I will always treasure it.

I believe that someone should never give up hope. I am in wrestling. This is my first year and I thought it would be easy. It is not easy but it is really fun.

In my first meet I won 2 out of 3 matches so I was happy. We have practice every day. And as much as I don't want to go, I want to do better in my meets so I go everyday and get my exercise. We have to give it all when we get in practice so we do good in our meets.

The last meet I was in, I didn't do so good. I didn't know why. So after the meet was over I wasn't looking at myself like I was a good wrestler but as I wrote this I realized that I can't give up hope in myself. Everyone has a bad day, so I can't beat myself up over one bad meet.

Everyone has got to have hope in what they're doing or you will never succeed. You can't do good if you don't think you can do good. So I believe that everyone needs to have hope. If you don't have hope at all how do you think you'll get better at something?

I believe in hope. Hope is to have desire in a certain expectation that you wish will happen or will be granted. If you're hopeful you'll get what is wanted. Hopeless is when you have no hope what-so-ever. But I believe that no one in the world is hopeless.

I once thought negatively and always doubted everything. I didn't believe in hope. So I didn't think I had hope in me. Throughout my elementary school years, I always prayed every night and hoped to have and find a best friend but every time I had a best friend I ended up loosing them within the year.

From kindergarten to 6th grade, I had a new set of friends each year. Then when middle school came along I remembered how I made a long prayer about friendship. I hoped that Sunrise Middle School would be different, both good and bad. I guess my mind told me to just give up already since I was "hopeless". Even when my heart told me to strive for the best. Middle school could change my life. It could be a turning point or the end of what was already "hopeless". I'd see everyone with their best friends here and there. Their other half, their second family. Someone they could lean and rely on. Someone they could vent to, be their true self and so much more.

I had no one. Seventh grade was going to be different but before I knew it I had already gave up on friendship. I doubted in everyone. I doubted in friendship. I even doubted in myself. One day I met this one guy that said something very important to me when we first met. I felt like he was my older brother. That sounds kind of corny but it was true! I told him about my problems – friendship problems. Then one day he said "every person you meet is a new door. You can't judge it from your past friendships". Now that was very touching to me. I took what he said to heart and I actually opened up to others more often. My hopes were high and I strived to find those who would stick by my side no matter what happens. Honestly, I think I found those type of friends. Until this day we are still best friends (more than over a year!). They are so much more than I can ever ask for.

I learned that regardless of what had happened in the past the future will be different if you make it happen. Having hope in yourself and others are important. Friends come and go. Best friends stay no matter how much struggle is happening, although you may struggle in finding your best and true friends. Hope will catch up to you soon. I believe in hope, everyone is hopeful and as long as they strive for the best, their wishes will come true. This I believe.

Hope is bringing light to the darkness and looking on the bright side. My cousin Mia Sanchez was four month's old when she got a deadly variation of meningitis. This variation makes your veins explode like balloons. It attacks you, your brain left ravaged. She was going through more pain than you, me and most of us will ever go through.

At first the doctors told us there was no hope, that the baby would be dead in less than 24 hrs. 24 hrs. flew by. My cousin got no better or worse. This time the doctors said 48 hrs., 72 hrs., 96 hrs. and finally 120 hrs. Then Mia started getting better and better. Due to her veins exploding all her blood rushed to the surface and her body got purple and black, just like a bruise. The doctors had to have a way to inject liquids into her body so they drilled a hole into her little spine.

Before her accident I used to think "ooh, a deadly disease, just get over it". But now I like to help people who are hurt. Mia remained in the ICU (intensive care unit) for over two months. Every year in the United States there are 4 or 5 cases of this illness a year and with luck one or two survive but with missing limbs and mental illness. My cousin survived with a perfect brain. She is very smart and only missing her little toe on her left foot. I believe in hope.

I believe in inspiring people. I believe Hope is bringing light to the darkness and looking on the bright side. The courage and the heart to do things better than they thought they could do.

What does the word inspire mean? To me it is one of the most important things that go on in ones life. When a person that you have been trying to impress or show them what you can do gives you a praise that gives you a surge of energy that can make you do greater things that you thought were impossible. This I believe…

During my season of cross-country I worked extremely hard to obtain my best time for the two mile course. My coach was strict but he also knew how to praise someone. During the run when you're almost finished he would come up to us and yell to us and to me. Once he did this I thought that I worked hard enough to beat my time and the person in front of me. This I believe.

What if no one considered his or her future? What if no one had hopes and beliefs inside of them? What if no one cared about what was going to happen next? The world would be filled with clueless people with no future ahead of them. None of us would know what we want to be when we grow up or have any goals. No one would have a cure for sickness or disease. No dreams, no wishes, no future. Nothing can go right and smooth without hope in the air.

Me, I've been one of those people that thought hopes and dreams would never come true and that life doesn't always give you what you want. I found out that I was wrong.

It all started a couple years ago in the second grade at Spring Mountain Elementary. I wasn't very wise and was pretty young then, but that doesn't matter. What matters is that I remember every second of those days. Well, I should say most of it. It makes me think back to that very moment, knowing I was very lucky.

During class I didn't feel very good and was often dizzy. I couldn't hear anything and just dozed off. I opened my eyes and found myself laying in bed with my mom by my side. What just happened? I had no idea. My mom explained to me how I threw up in class and she took me home. What scared me was that I had no idea that happened. I didn't remember anything.

As my mom went to get me some medicine to drink, once again, I dozed off and everything turned pitch black. I didn't know why or how. I opened my eyes, not finding myself in bed this time, but in an ambulance.

I stayed at the Children's Hospital at Legacy Emanuel as the doctors ran tests. Unfortunately they never found out what disease I had and didn't know how to treat me, not even why or how this happened. My family was very frightened because of what I had was unknown. I had to stay at the hospital for quite some time until I felt better, but who knew when that would be? All we were able to do was hope for the best.

At that moment my mind was concentrating on feeling better and was counting on our beliefs. I had visitors everyday, such as my family and friends. That made me realize that all of these people cared for me.

As the days went by I began feeling worse. When someone would touch me it felt as if I was burning on that one section of my skin. I wasn't able to walk either. I didn't understand any of this back then or what was happening. I still don't know.

My mom then began to worry, so she left to go to church and pray for a cure. My aunt watched over me as my mom was gone. She thought that maybe if I took a stroll around the hospital I'd feel better. So that is what I did. I held onto my wheel chair handles as my aunt held onto my hand even though it burned. All of a sudden I felt better. The burning feeling went away in a flash and I was able to walk after the next day. I guess my mom and all of the other's prayers came true.

Now I know that hopes and dreams do come true. I was wrong and this moment of my life made me believe. I now value compassion, family members, friends, and most importantly hope. I believe hope is what gets us to keep going and what guides our lives for the better. Hope is what creates a future.

    I believe hope can help you through the most difficult things in life. My grandma is the strongest person I know. She is what you would call a "tough cookie". When I was six years old I found out my grandma had been diagnosed with breast cancer. Even though I was barely past Kindergarten I can remember this part of my life vividly because it changed me a lot. Hearing about cancer on T.V. and from my parents, I never imagined it would hit my family. I felt scared and sad and angry all at the same time. Seeing my grandma go to countless doctor appointments, lose all of her hair from the chemo and have to buy a wig tore me up inside. When I talked to my mom, she told me that all we could do was hope and pray that my grandma would recover. I hoped and hoped for about a year and a half. It was really hard, but once I had hope in my life it made it much easier to struggle through her recovery. Like I said, my grandma is a tough cookie. She had the easiest time out of all of us. My grandma started getting better and when I was seven years old she had recovered from cancer. Everyone in my family was relieved and happy. I believe that hope can get you through any hard time. My grandma has been cancer-free for six years. Anytime you are struggling hope can help you through it. THIS I BELIEVE.

    I believe in hope. To look forward to something with confidence and expectation is a good feeling and sometimes it's the only thing people have.

    My family's friend, Kris, was very close to us. One day we found out that she had cancer. We were all devastated. My family, including my aunts and uncles, decided to help her out to the best of our ability. We took a big plastic sign to people we knew her that said, "you can do it Kris!" We then took a picture with them. We even took pictures with people we didn't know. After awhile we made an album full of pictures saying – you can do it Kris! We even had a hat party where we gave her a bunch of hats to wear because all of her hair was gone. We hoped that she would make it through. Kris was very unique. She was a runner. She took part in the Hood to Coast and other running events. She also had two cats and three dogs. Two of her animals only had one eye. She even created a walking group that walked or ran every Saturday and everyone would get coffee afterwards. Later on Kris's daughter Kara was also diagnosed with cancer. Kris and Kara then fought cancer together. Unfortunately Kris passed away on Halloween of 2009. Her daughter Kara continues to fight cancer with all of our support. I believe that hope is a powerful thing. Hope is what got all of us through. I am still hoping that Kara gets rid of her cancer, all of us are. Kris's husband Dan probably hoped the most. We have Dan over for dinner every once in awhile because he is lonely. Hope can get you through everything. This I believe.

What does hope mean to you? Does it mean to hope for something good to happen? Or even just make it through your life? Hope means never give up until you finish what you started. This I believe.

When I was 5 yrs. old I dreamed of playing sports until the end of forever. But before I could live my dream, heart surgery got in my way. If I never had the heart surgery I wouldn't be playing sports today. Up until the heart surgery I had the hardest time breathing. Every time I went back to the hospital I would hope to get better. I would hope to play sports. I never stopped hoping. My family hoped for me, the doctors and friends. They all hoped I would come out a new person. If I never had hoped I would still have the heart problems. I never would of came out to finish what I started in life. We should all hope to move through life finishing a piece of our goal, to make it to our dream. Just never stop hoping until you finish what you started. Now, until this day, every time I hear the word hope, I think of my heart surgery and the story behind it.

I believe that there is always hope for my future. This year I did CIS, a career information system. This made me remember when I was little and people would always ask me what I wanted to be. I was crazy about climbing, so of course I would say proudly "I want to be a professional climber!" While I started CIS I knew that I wouldn't be able to do that. I searched through occupations looking for something that I would enjoy. I came across an Internist, a doctor that works with patients who have an illness that doesn't require surgery. The problem is I've never been good at science. It is one of the main subjects it has to do with. I love science, I'm just not the best at it. My grandfather is a doctor. He has always pushed me to do my best and to find something that makes me happy. He is a very giving man and loves his career very much. My mother would tell me countless times to get off what I was climbing. I would never stop because I loved it so much. In the beginning I wasn't very good at climbing but since I had such a strive for it, I kept climbing and climbing. If I do that with science I could become very strong in it. When I would climb the fence in my backyard I would sit on top of it and look at the blue sky. I now sit in a science room looking at the same blue sky as before and see my dreams. I believe that there is always hope for my future.

I believe in hope. Hope is the key to survival. There are certain things people need. Food, clothes, water and shelter. We also need hope. Hope is one of the few things that keeps someone going like a boat on a creek. Sometimes the sun will try to dry the creek up leaving the boat in the dirt until the rain comes and refills the stream with new water.

I personally know what it's like to feel hopeless. You feel empty like your going to fall and nothing is there to catch you. The world seems to collapse around you and even the love of your family at times isn't enough. I felt this way when I moved a few weeks ago. I had to leave almost everything behind. My family and friends were so far away that I'd only be able to see them every now and then. When I first found out that we were going to move I felt as if the floor beneath me vanished and that I would never be able to stop falling towards despair. This is the feeling of hopelessness. The saying "having the rug pulled out beneath your feet" isn't just a saying. It's a feeling. You can see the walls spinning around you. Hopelessness is a terrifying, dangerous feeling a person can actually get lost in and sometimes it's the next thing to impossible to get them out. Hope is the only way to free yourself. Whatever the trial is that you're going through – the death of a family member or being teased because you can't do something right. Hope can and will get you through it. I do my best even though I'm shy to help people that are hopeless. There are people that understand you. All you have to do is look for them. This I believe.

One day in February, I was so pre-occupied with my birthday, which was in three days. But as I woke up, about to get ready for school, I received a text from my sister asking if I wanted to go to California but we would have to leave right away. So naturally I said yes, very excited thinking nothing was wrong. A few minutes later she called me saying the trip wasn't a vacation.

Listening to her crying made me worried and scared. My grandma was dying and almost did that day. My sister pulled my brother and sister out of school on a Wednesday morning and we drove straight to California. My dad had already been there for about a week, but didn't tell us exactly why, but that day we knew. I never felt more scared and anxious at the same time and not knowing what to expect or how I should react to what I see.

We stayed in California until Monday. Helping and spending all the time with my grandma. Lots of people were coming in and out of the house to see her. Everyone besides my cousins left my dad, and they started to talk to me about death and what was going on and how everything was going to happen. It was very uncomfortable. I tried not to cry but tears just ran down my face faster than they ever had before. I sat there silently listening. The day we left I had to say goodbye but I had no idea how to so I acted like normal and said I'll see her next time. I didn't even know if there was going to be a next time. I realized spending time with the ones you love before it's too late can mean the world to someone. A few days later I received a picture message from my dad of a picture of my grandma feeding herself. I heard lots of good news. So far, even off all her medication, my grandma was improving. It may not seem like much but to the ones who saw her before it's like a miracle. And because of this I believe in hope because no matter how bad things seem it can always get better and no one knows what will happen next.

I believe in hope. I believe in hope because hope always gets you somewhere good in life. When your sick or sad you always hope that you will get better, by hoping it will happen. Hope is the feeling in your heart that something better will happen in the future.

I moved to the United States because my family hoped that it would be better here than Russia. We had to move because the government didn't let Christians live. Policemen would come to random houses and if they saw bibles they would burn them and put people in jail for their religion. People had hope that everything would get better in the future but it was getting worse everyday.

Then lots of people started moving away to a different countries. We had hope that America would allow our religion there and that we could start going to church again instead of hiding every weekend to have church. So we moved to the United States to have freedom for our religion.

All I am trying to say here is that everyone believes in hope. Hope is all around us. Sometimes we don't even notice what's going on in the present time. We could never live without hope helping us along the way. Wherever you go or whatever you do hope will always follow you.

I believe in hope because everyone needs hope to do important things in life. One time I was at a private school and everyone hated me because of my style. But one person didn't hate me, she was the only person that had hope for me. One time the school went to the ropes course in Salem and everyone said the course was scary. I was scared to go up on the zip line, but she had hope and gave me courage by saying,"Just go, you can do it, I know you can." I was scared, but I had courage and went for it. The zip line was the most fun I ever had in a long time. That's why I believe in hope for those things to happen. If anyone has hope in you or you have courage, go for it. Now when I see other people who have hope in me or other people, it makes me think of that time when she helped me. She was so kind, nice, sweet and gave me the hope and courage that I needed. For that I feel like she is a sister to me just because she was the only one who had hope in me. I believe in hope.

When I was in first grade I found out that my right kidney had failed and shriveled up. Many times this would bring me pain. So on November 4, 2004 I had to go to the hospital and get it removed. I was terrified when it was time to go in. Right before it started, I started to think to myself that this would change who I am and that I would never be the same.

When the surgery was over, I was so relived but I was also so scared that something would go wrong. Many days passed, my parents and many others all hoped that I would be okay and heal properly. Knowing that people cared for me and that they had high hopes for me to be okay taught me to be hopeful. I should be hopeful even when thing are hard and seem to have hit rock bottom. You can never give up and must always look to the bright side of things. I believe in hope. This I believe.

Hope

I believe that hope is a very strong word. At a young age of 7, I played soccer.

Since I was at a young age there was only one defender on the soccer field at a time. All of my teammates called me "The Boot". They called me that because I could kick the soccer ball the farthest on the team.

During soccer games I would play as the defender in almost every game. When I played as a defender I would play for almost the whole game. Whenever the other team tried to score a goal I would almost always stop them.

As the offense on the other team was running up the field my teammates and I would hope that I would stop the offense on the other team from scoring a goal. Whenever we all hoped that I would stop them, it always seemed that it kept the other team from scoring.

When I stopped the other team from scoring, all of the parents on our team were shouting with joy!

Even though I don't play soccer anymore, I always think back to those days as a young soccer player and have hope in myself. It always gives me a positive outlook on my life.

    I believe in hope. You need to be optimistic about life and the things that happen. I came to realize this when my aunt had preclampsia (a form of toxemia in pregnancy, characterized by hypertension, fluid retention and albuminuria, sometimes progressing to eclampsia). The worst part of it all is that she was pregnant with my little baby cousin, Lucia. I woke up one radiant morning, getting ready for church. Walking around the house, I saw that my mom was gone. I asked my dad where my mom had gone to and he responded that she was in the hospital with my aunt. He explained that my cousin had been born. A smile spread across my face, but it was washed away. My dad began to sob. At first I thought it was tears of joy, but I could see the pain in his eyes.

    I was getting anxious. When my dad stopped crying he continued with the rest of the story. "Your aunt's liver got so swollen that it hit one of her ribs and she began to bleed internally. They had to get Lucia out so the doctors could make the bleeding stop. Your mom is coming home soon so we call all go to the hospital." I began to feel this great misery in my heart. Not long after, I as well, start to mourn. At that moment I wanted to go back to sleep because my dreams were better than real life.

    I ran to my brother's room to tell him we needed to get dressed. I could tell he knew what was happening because his cheeks were still wet from his tears. Once we all got ready, I could hear a door close shut. It was my mom. She flew across the kitchen and hugged us all. My mom told us that my aunt's liver kept on bleeding, but my little cousin was fine. We all rushed to the car and headed to the hospital. I nervously thought to myself, what would the doctor tell us when we got there?

When we arrived at the hospital, my cousins were also there. I ran towards them and we all embraced each other. We walked to the elevator, hoping the doctor would give us good new. Finally, we entered the waiting room and our whole family was there, supporting my aunt. Most of them were smiling and laughing quietly. How could they be happy in a dark siltation like this?

Then it occurred to me that their hearts must be filled with hope, hope that my aunt and cousin were going to be in good health. I prayed in my heart that the light of hope could brighten this dark circumstance. Not long after, the doctor came and told us the bleeding had stopped. We all rejoiced with happiness and I could feel the warmth of hope reassuring me that all was going to be well. I believe that if life gives you a hundred reasons to cry, you can show life you have a thousand reason to smile.

It took my aunt some weeks to recover, but now-a-days, she's the jolliest mom and aunt ever! And for my cousin,she's a little bundle of joy. I believe that no one know what's going to happen tomorrow. Life is a crazy ride and nothing is guaranteed. You just need to hope for the best and the best just might happen. This, I believe.

"Hope seems invisible, feels intangible and achieves impossible." This quote has inspired me greatly when I was going through tough times. Even when you think there's completely nothing, there's always hope. I had times when I wanted to give up on everything. I felt like I was alone in a dark empty room. The first time I felt like that was in the fifth grade. In fifth grade, my teacher told my class to write about our favorite place to go on a vacation to. I chose to write about Cancun, Mexico. It's beautiful and a wonderful place to go on a vacation to. The hotel I stayed in was a 4 star hotel, it was simply amazing. Now, I can write or describe how amazing Cancun was but back then in fifth grade, I couldn't.

My family speaks a foreign language and I do too. My parents couldn't help me with most of my homework that required reading and writing because their English was not good. Neither was mine, but I didn't like asking for help so I did all of my homework by myself. Although I read at my grade level, writing an essay was extremely hard for me. When I had to start writing my rough draft, my mind suddenly became a piece of clean and white paper. I was s struggling with a piece of clean paper for hours. It was depressing. I couldn't even write a word because I had no idea how to write the very first sentience or "hook".

However, at that moment, writing essays wasn't the only thing on my mind. In my mind, I was blaming my parents for my poor English. If my parents spoke English, I wouldn't have been struggling to write a simple essay. Confused and lost, I couldn't stop the tears from running down my face. However, I eventually stopped crying

Hope

because I realized that crying wouldn't help me finish the essay I didn't even start on. Also, I realized that if I tried hard to make the essay perfect, then I'd really be perfect. Therefore, I was determined to finish the essay and try my best on other things too. I believe it was hope that made me be optimistic and determined

Now I know that there's always hope, I'll be always bright and optimistic. Also, my goal is to live my life to the fullest and be happy and hopeful everyday. Remember, hope can be the most powerful thing in the world.

I believe in hope. When you're young you think all kids and people, for the most part, are the same. Well that's what I thought before I realized, as I grew older, my sister wasn't the same.

My sister is 10 years old and she has a syndrome called Rubinstein Syndrome (RTS). It's a pretty rare genetic disorder that keeps her brain from fully developing. It's as if she is actually 7 years old today and will continue to develop slower than most kids.

I am inspired by her because she keeps trying to overcome things that people say she can't do and I hope this is something she never loses. She can easily be challenged by things we sometimes take for granted but she doesn't give up! She just says "myself" and keeps on trying by herself.

Whenever I feel like giving up, I think of my sister, her consistent positive attitude which will forever inspire me to keep going today and throughout my adult life.

I will always believe that anything is possible, nobody is exactly the same, and our differences are what makes us unique.

I HOPE as my sister grows older that this part of her will never change.

I believe having hope is the best way to get through tough situations. When I was 7 years old, my grandma had dementia. She came to live with us because she couldn't be alone at her own house. This was very hard to adjust to because we only had 4 bedrooms. My parents in theirs, my sister in hers, my brother in his and my grandma would sleep in mine. So I had to sleep in my 2 years old brother's room with him. The biggest issue with this new arrangement was that my grandma didn't act like herself, or even her age. She would fight with my brother like they were siblings, and insist that she drink out of a sippy cup. Having her change like this was hard on us all. We didn't give up on her though. My dad found her a retirement home to live in after she'd been staying with us for almost 3 months. They took care of her there and she made friends. We would notice her getting better, acting more normal, more like her old self. Now she's been at her retirement home for all these years. We bring her to our house to see her about once every week or two. She comes over and plays board games and tells us stories about her life. Sometimes it's like she never had changed at all. We had hope and got through tis situation. This is why I've come to believe having hope is the best way to get through tough situations

I believe in the power of hope.

The event I am going to describe is when I started learning how to play the violin. It happened when I was 9 years old in Portland, Oregon at Classique Music Academy. My mom and my music teacher were both involved in motivating me to play the violin.

There were so many thoughts going through my head that day. I was scared, nervous, excited, happy and glad. When I think back to that day, I feel proud of myself because I started to learn how to play the violin. At first I was scared and thought maybe this is not for me but then it hit me, I can do it.

My music teacher said that there is nothing to be scared of, and so did my mom. After my first lesson I felt proud of myself because I learned the names of the strings, and how to hold the bow properly. At that moment I had hope. Hope that one day I could become a good violin player.

Now I have been playing the violin for 3 full years. Playing the violin brings me joy. As a violin player I have lots of hope and I have a dream of being a very good violin player. I believe that one day, maybe I will even become a famous player. This I believe!

On April 7, 2009, I was horribly sick with an undiagnosed illness. My dad, who is a paramedic, was worried about my heavy breathing and sunken eyes. Something bad was happening and it needed to be dealt with quickly. My did swept me up, as my body was eating me alive, and took me to the ER. Turns out my blood glucose was 400 over average. At that point my life changed forever.

April 8, 2009 at 2:30 am I was diagnosed as a type 1 diabetic. From that point on I had to give myself 4 shots a day and check my sugar every 3 hours. I started to think about what my friends, family, teachers and instructors would think about my new life as a type 1. Would they think I'm broken or that I was unhealthy? Those thoughts scared me until April 9, 2009. I finally left the hospital and was ready to get home. As I opened the front door there were cards, balloons, flowers, posters, teddy bears, and pictures sitting there, waiting for this tiny little diabetic girl to be cheered up. I swear, the smile on my face curled into my ears. I felt so comforted reading all the sweet notes written by fellow students, close families and of course all my friends! At that moment I realized something that I would never forget. Life can be lifeless, hopeless, unbelievable, unimportant and misread sometimes. But I believe when life is being questioned, you're the one really being questioned. I believe making mistakes or going through tough times is just a detour on the road. You will get back on the street eventually after getting through the delay. I believe getting back on track is just on puzzle piece closer to discovering your life. Take the detour, and get to your destination. This I believe.

I believe life is short so we should live everyday like it was our last. I was twelve years old, taking a trip to California with my mom, my two older brothers, and my great grandma. We were going to stay with our aunt Jean, my great grandma's sister and go to Disneyland and California Adventures during the day.

The first couple of days were great. We rode our favorite rides and went back to the house and got a good night of rest. Then about 5:30 AM, my mom got a call. It was her step-mom, she was sobbing.

"Becky, it's your dad..."

"What? What happened?" Mom said panicky.

"Last night, we were at my work party, having a good time, smiling laughing and dancing. The next thing I knew he had a heart attack." she said bawling.

"What?" was all my mom could say, she was crying now.

"A massive heart attack, he..." she hesitated, "He passed away."

They both were weeping now.

My mom got off the phone and went to tell my great grandma, his mom. The same thing happened, except she took it worse. Mom let us sleep in a couple more hours, then as word got around, people started calling. My mom didn't want us to find out by over hearing someone so she woke us up. She told my brothers and I, and we started crying for what felt like hours. I went outside and started to comfort my great grandma. She and Aunt Jean told me that they talked to him the day before. They told him how my brothers and I wished we could spend more time with him.

He replied, "Alright Mom, trust me. I will be spending a lot more time with them. And do me a favor. Make sure and tell them I love them for me."

Of course they did, and inside me I could feel my grandpa was with us, right there with us. I lifted my head up towards the sky.

"I love you too." I said smiling.

Jack McAllister – February 14, 1948 – December 20, 2009.

When I realize how short life can be I remember to start living everyday like it's my last. This I believe.

I believe that everything happens for a reason. Sometimes that reason doesn't reveal itself for years, but every once in a while the timing is profound. I came to really understand this six years ago while working at an Italian restaurant.

Throughout high school and college, many of the jobs that I had involved food service. My first summer job was at a snack bar at a community swimming pool, I later worked in a mess hall at a summer camp, and was also a short order cook my freshman year in college. That being said, I was quite comfortable working in the food service industry. Six years ago I found myself once again serving food, this time as a waiter. It had been five years since I had graduated from college, and my degree was as valuable as a raincoat in the Sahara. After spending the last two years selling cars, I knew that I needed to find a career. The restaurant wasn't a career for me by any means, but it would allow me to go back to graduate school and earn another degree.

I wasn't sure exactly what I should earn my degree in, but I knew that I wanted to remove myself from jobs that led nowhere, had no benefits, and were merely a means to a paycheck. I thought about law school for sometime, but wasn't sure that I wanted to spend three years preparing for a career that I may or may not be truly passionate about. My wife had recently been certified as a teacher, and education was my other consideration. After mulling it over for a few weeks, I decided on applying to Concordia University, to attend their M.A.T. program, and become a high school social studies teacher.

So there I was, recently removed from the wonderful world of new and used automobile sales, and back in the old food service game. My application had been sent off for about a month, and I waited anxiously to hear if I was to be accepted to the program and was about to change my career path.

My first night on the job was not unlike many of the other first nights as a waiter. Different specials to remember, new systems for ordering, a new crazy chef that like to yell and swear when the dinner rush hit; all were par for the course. Being my first night, I was only given one or two tables at a time, and all in all things went well. I can't recall that anyone was dissatisfied with my service, as I struggled with saying different Italian words that were new to me: "car bon air a, mont a pull chiano, etc."

Nothing was out of the ordinary until a nice couple in their 30's was ready for their bill.

The woman told me that she ran a dance studio, worked with kids on a daily basis, and loved being a teacher. She also said, after prefacing that she didn't mean to sound strange, but that she and her husband had been discussing how they thought that I would make a good teacher. They had no knowledge that I was waiting to hear from the university if I was accepted or not. Once I told them this, they both laughed at the coincidence and I wished them a good night. It was a pleasant start to a new job that seemed to be a good fit for me.

It wasn't until they were leaving that the coincidence started seeming like destiny. The woman took me aside, told me that she never did this sort of thing, but wanted to give me a $100 tip, and to follow my dreams. A pretty nice start to a new job, but it was only the icing. When I opened my mailbox the next afternoon my acceptance letter was waiting for me. Everything happens for a reason, this I believe.

-Staff

I believe we should not look at life by how many days we live but how we live each day.

When my grandparents walked into the room at their 50th anniversary, the smile on their faces were almost ear to ear, and the water in their eyes said it all. All that moment there was no need for words. I silently thought to myself, would I be this happy when I am old? As it grew louder, I knew that today this was the right place to be and I was with the right people. People who loved and cared for me, I knew that's how we should spend each day.

That day went on and my grandparents told us stories of when they were young. I knew I should cherish everyday and live as each one was my last. No one had to tell me it wasn't easy. My grandma and grandpa didn't live an easy life back in Russia, where they were punished for their beliefs. They just didn't spend much time worrying about it but just moved on.

That day taught me many things. I learned that you don't always get a second chance to patch things up. Living each day to the fullest, doing the unexpected, and helping the people you haven't helped. As I think about and relive that day, I know now I'll never regret doing the right thing and making it my best. This I Believe.

Towards the end of the year in seventh grade, I took a simple, ten question quiz in my social studies class. Two days later, my teacher handed back the quiz. I looked at the top of my paper and saw "9/10, 90%, A", written in red ink with a happy face next to it. " One point isn't too bad," I thought. Then I looked over the rest of my paper to see where I had gone wrong. " This isn't right," I thought as I examined my paper. I had seen "-1" written twice instead of once like I expected. I checked over my notes and found that I had indeed answered both questions incorrectly. I know that if I told my teacher, I would lose my A and get a B instead. But I also knew that "honesty is the best policy", and that I should show some honesty. So I did, and I felt proud of myself. Even though I had lost my A, it still felt good because I knew I had shown that I was honest enough to show my teacher her mistake. I believe in honesty because even though the result isn't always good, the result always ends up good. I believe in honesty, and I believe that everyone should be honest.

I believe that integrity is important because trustworthiness is important in any relationship or friendship. Most people have been told at a very young age not to lie. Most people know that lying is bad and they will be punished. Most people have been told that lying behind someone's back is almost worse than lying to their face. But most people do it anyway. I learned in the second grade how to have integrity.

Back in the second grade, everybody who was anybody was into the game of Yu-gi-oh. This is how I got into trouble with my parents for not having integrity. My brother, who was in kindergarten at the time, was also very into Yu-gi-oh. He purchased three rare cards from a friend and I was unlucky enough to find out about it. My parents were not told that he had done this and I told my brother that I wouldn't tell if he gave me one of these cards. My brother ended up getting caught for this but he didn't rat me out....for a while.

That next day was a great day until nighttime came along. That was when my parents asked my brother why he did it, and that was when I got in trouble. I learned that day that lying is bad, but not coming out and telling the truth when you are hiding something is just as bad. Sometimes punishment can help one realize what they did wrong and can help them change in the process. Integrity...This I Believe.

    I believe that honesty is the most important thing that keeps a relationship together. If no one in the world believes that honesty is important, then there would be no friendship. No one would trust each other, and lots of people would cheat and lie. A friendship without honesty is like a flower with no petals.

    For example, when I was in kindergarten, I met a girl named Katie. We always got along and never had big fights. We were best friends, and always did everything together. Until one day in third grade, Katie told me that she didn't want to be my best friend. This hurt me, I didn't know what to do. She had been my only close friend, I had no one else to turn to.

    When me and my friends are really close, I sometimes worry that I might loose them. I have learned from this experience because I now know that I have to stick up for myself and tell my friends how I feel. I need to tell them if I am mad at them for something, or even if I am sad and I need encouragement. Honesty is very important to have in a good relationship.

    I believe in honesty. Lies are a part of us but so is honesty. If everyone lies then no one will know the truth of what happened. When I was around 7 or 8, my dad had a talk with me and my sister. It was summer time, we were sitting on the couch. It was dark because we closed the blinds. My dad said that if we lie that we didn't do anything, sooner or later people will find out. And when they do, you would be in deeper trouble unless you tell us the truth first. Back then, I felt like a bad boy being lectured. But now, I know my dad was trying to help me be an honest man. Before my dad told me about honesty, I thought lying would make the problems go away. Now that I know it doesn't, being honest about breaking the flower vase is better than lying about it. I would be punished but not as bad as when I lie. I wanted my parents to love me when I was young. They do but I want to make them happy so I don't lie and don't break valuable stuff in our house. I still lie today, but not as much as I used to before my dad told me about honesty. My father taught me a valuable lesson that day. Now I believe honesty is the better way to go than going on the path of lying. Thanks dad.

I believe in honesty and integrity. I was the child in our family who would lie just to get out of trouble. I hurt people when I lied. I hurt myself when I lie. I hurt my family when I lied.

I kept having these dreams that right before my mom died, the last thing I told her was a lie. These dreams really hit me hard and made me think about what I have been doing. I realized that the lies I told don't just go away. They stick with me. The guilt of lying is such a heavy emotion that it breaks you down piece by piece, even if it's something as simple as lying about a homework assignment. These dreams really changed me. I now know that the consequences of your actions are not as bad as the guilt of lying. Sure I could get away with it but that is not the point. I now try to never lie. If I do lie, I feel so bad about it that I go and tell whoever I lied to that I lied and I give them the truth. The power of guilt can really change a person's life. It has completely turned my life around. Telling the truth really makes me feel good even if I do have to face the consequences for my actions. This whole experience of changing my life has made me happier and glad. I get to live life without any guilt and be a normal, honest teenager. For this reason I believe in Honesty and Integrity.

    I believe in honesty to your family. I was lying to my dad for two years. He didn't even notice until he saw my report card. He didn't know what to do, so he gave me a two to three hour lecture about how I shouldn't lie to my family. Then I realized honesty is better than getting in trouble. So he grounded me for the rest of the year, but it was only two months. He also told me always tell the truth. When I was getting a lecture, I remembered all the good times he and I had and how much fun we have together. I was so sad how I treated my dad. So I made a promise that I will never lie to my dad again. I believe in honesty to your family because the truth is better than lying.

Integrity

I believe in honesty because telling the truth is always the right thing to do instead of lying about the things you do.

I'm in 8th grade, and it was my lunchtime. I was trying to trip two others and that day was horrible. The lunchroom was noisy, loud and crowded. I thought it would be funny, but I know that I should not trip people because it's not safe. Mr. H. told me not to lie to him so I told the truth. Lying is not the way to go because lying will get you in more trouble than telling the truth, and being honest to all the adults. Telling the truth is better than lying because it feels good. I believe in honesty because it feels good to tell the truth.

    I believe in honesty, even if there are consequences. Honesty has always been important to me, but it wasn't until one day in my orchestra class that I realized just how important honesty could be. Telling the truth almost always solves my problems.

    Once-upon-a-fourth-period, I was in orchestra. My violin's "D" string was severely out of tune. I couldn't fix it, so I decided to have my teacher(Mrs. Lorimor) tune it for me. Then disaster struck. Being a bit klutzy is usual for me, but usually I am not holding something when I trip. So when I tripped on a cable, the object in my hands fell to the ground. The object in my hands was....my violin!!!

    There was a loud "thump" and the classroom quieted down. A group of "oohs" could be heard as I said, "Everything is fine." My words had made everybody go back to whatever they were doing. However, I knew that my violin was not fine.

    When I got home, all that I could stare at was the gynormous crack along the front of my violin. I was in complete panic mode. How was I going to tell my parents? Can my violin be fixed or would I have to get a new one? Those questions swam inside my every thought for the next few days, until finally the day had come.

    I had made a resolution to tell my parents. Now I just had to go through with it. Easier said than done. My eyelids squeezed together, and I blurted out,"My violin has a crack in it, 'cause I dropped it." I peeked out of one eye and then the other. Complete silence filled the room.

    After my parents recovered from their shock, and my

little sister said "someone's in trouble", I retold the whole story. Luckily my parents didn't seem too mad (maybe a bit grouchy). The very next day, we went to the violin store. I moved up a violin size and said "hello" to my new violin.

Honesty is always the answer. Sometimes honesty has bad effects, but mostly good effects come out of telling the truth. Honesty is always the right thing to do, even if there are consequences, this I believe.

    I believe in integrity. I believe in it because in third grade my friend showed me integrity. Integrity is doing the right thing when no one is watching. One day when we were in the library checking out our books, and on our way to class a twenty dollar bill fell from her book. When she was bending down to pick it up, I thought she was going to keep it for herself. Suddenly she walks back into the library. When she comes back to the classroom and sits down next to me she tells me what happened. Apparently she gave the money back to the librarian and told her to give it to the person who had the book last. The librarian was apparently surprised and she gave my friend a lollipop. I have lots of respect for my friend, and I have learned to do what she has shown me.

I believe that anyone, and everyone, can show integrity. Integrity is doing the right thing even when no one is watching. Whether it be the science teacher that seems to hate your guts, helping at a soup kitchen, the bully who has never once cheated on a test, or maybe the homeless men that find shelter in the library. This is where my story begins.

It was just your average day here in Oregon, cold and rainy. I was at the library. I had just watched a movie called "Pay It Forward" and was on a total "pay it forward" kick, so that was why I was at the library. For those of you who don't know what paying it forward is, here it is in a nutshell--when someone does something nice for you, instead of paying them back, you pay it forward and do something nice for someone else. (I am also a strong believer in paying it forward). So any way, I was going to give doughnuts to the homeless that basically live at the library. My goal was the abandoned shopping cart parked outside. It was filled with all of their worldly possessions and they had left it unguarded, or so it seemed. I knew that at least one of them had to be watching me creeping ever so close to their belongings, so I moved quickly, and maybe a little too rushed, knowing that they would be there soon to see what I'd left. I dashed away just as one of them got to the cart. As I drove away the smile on his face was the biggest reward ever. Who knew how much joy a box of "Krispy Kremes" could bring to someone who wasn't even eating them. But my story doesn't end there.

That morning, I awoke to a phone call offering a trip to the movies with my friends Kendra and Jordan. I scrambled around trying to find my purse. But it was nowhere to be found. That purse came from a yard sale and had my birthday money in it. I knew just where it was. With little hope of retrieval, I slumped back to the library. Even though I had given doughnuts to the homeless, I had them written off as convicts and slums. Knowing they needed the money more than I ever would, I was positive they had stolen it. So I went to the librarian and asked if anyone had turned in a purse. She reached behind her and picked up just about the only purse in the world with feet...my purse! She just sort of smiled and I knew who had turned it in. Not gonna lie, they were terrible actors, pretending to read as they watched us. Grins spread across everyone of their faces.

That day I learned to believe in integrity. You better believe I checked that purse's contents up and down. Nothing, not a cent, had been taken. Anyone can show integrity, and almost everyone does. This I believe.

I believe in integrity. I believe that people should be treated fairly. There was an event in sixth grade that involved me showing integrity. This happened at my old school called "Christ the King", at recess. It involved some kids in our class picking on and making fun of this kid at recess. When I saw what they were doing, I felt angry and annoyed. However, I felt good about myself that I stood up for this kid. Before this event ever took place, I was afraid that people would get mad at me for standing up for this guy. But after this happened, I now know that I can stand up for people. Back then, I valued the importance of doing the right thing all the time. And even to this day I still value the importance of doing the right thing all the time.

    I believe that it is important for everyone to show integrity. Last week I was at the mall shopping for jewelry. I was in a store that sold foreign things from different countries. There were some beautiful Indian rings for sale for only $2.00. So I decided to grab a handful. While I was walking around looking at the rest of the stuff I accidentally slipped one of the rings on my finger without noticing, then I just bought my other items and casually left the store. It wasn't until about an hour later that I noticed the unpaid for ring innocently wrapped around my finger. At first I was a little startled because I had never even considered stealing anything before. Then I thought nothing of it because after all, the ring was only $2.00. So I decided to leave it at that and get on with my shopping. While I was walking around I couldn't' shake the feeling that I had done something extremely wrong. I felt like somehow everyone in the stores knew what I had done and they were all silently judging me. In the back of my mind I was telling myself to forget about it, it was no big deal and just move on, but I couldn't help feeling so selfish and disgusted with myself. After awhile I couldn't take the guilt anymore, so I quickly hurried back to the store that I took the ring from. When I got there a terrifying feeling washed over me, and I was too scared to approach the man working at the front desk. I thought he would be really angry at me for stealing from the store. I decided to be brave. I slowly walked up to the counter and immediately apologized for taking the ring. The man thanked me for my honesty, then he started chuckling because the ring was only $2.00, but in the end I know that integrity is priceless. This I Believe.

I believe in doing what's right.

"Be quiet," my friend, Matt whispered. We cautiously threw one roll over the house. Then we tossed another in the tree. As we threaded the paper in and out of their property we noticed a light in their house. The three of us decided it would be best to stay low.

After a few more minutes the prank was complete and we ran as far away as possible. Chris, my other friend said, "I think we'll get caught."

"No we won't, " Matt argued.

"My dad," whispered Chris, "would kill me if he know!"

Jokingly Matt said, "Fine, you want us to go all the way back and take all of the toilet paper down?"

"Yes," Chris said bluntly. I even felt guilty inside, but I decided to stay out of it.

Five minutes later, and we're back at the house. Once again, the three of us snuck around their property. This time when we were at the house, we picked up every scrap of paper. I could tell Matt reluctantly picked up the toilet paper, but he still did it.

That night I learned that everyone should do the right thing. Even thought we did something bad to start with, it turned out we did a good deed to make up for it (since it was like we were never there). I believe in doing what's right.

    I believe that people truly want to do the right thing. I'll admit that I am not a very organized person. I am constantly checking my pockets to make sure my phone, iPod or money is still there. It can be kind of scary to lose something of high importance. To feel your eyes widen, your heartbeat race and your body temperature drop is very surreal. It's always good to know that there is someone on your side, even in one of your most vulnerable states.

    When you lose something, you are sometimes quick to blame others. I believe that integrity is sometimes very rare. To know that someone is going to go out of their way to return something that they could easily just take, really show that they care. When I was at a convention hosted at a hotel, it was a very exciting atmosphere. There was a dance, games and overall, a circus in the main hall of the hotel. As I sat down to play a game, I quickly lost and picked up my stuff to leave. Three steps later, OCD stepped in and I started to check my pockets. As the blood drained from my face and an icy shiver went down my back, I started to hunt for my phone. After rechecking the game area, a younger kid approached me asking if I had lost my phone. He returned it. I felt mixed emotions about his accident because usually when I lose something, I never proceed to find it.

    Knowing that there is someone who wants to help makes a big difference in the way you think and act every day. I believe that everyone truly wants to do the right thing. Sometimes they just have to be shown how. Usually it's hard to do the right thing. I believe in integrity because sometimes doing the right thing has a greater pay out then taking the easy way out. Deep down I know that people want to do the right thing. As little kids, all you want to do is give, not take. As you get older, some of your innocence is stripped away and all you do is take. Sometimes if you want to do the right thing, you have to be reminded of your innocence and powered by your youth. As a kid, you have much to learn from adults. As an adult, you have much to learn from kids.

    I believe in integrity. This all started when I was in middle school. I was eating my lunch just like I do everyday. All of my friends were there and we were just talking and having fun. Some of the people at the table were trying to get me to say things that I don't think are right. I felt like I was being betrayed by them because they knew what I thought about the subject. I was very nervous and scared because I thought if I didn't say what they wanted me to say, they wouldn't be my friends anymore. Looking back on it, I still feel like I made the right decision and did exactly what I thought and knew was right. For me, it is very important to not give into negative peer pressure. It doesn't matter if anyone is watching, if you think it is wrong, chances are it is. I now know that peers can try to pressure you into doing things that you know are wrong and that they still try just to see if they can break you. Not letting bad words come out of my mouth has always been a very important value. Now that I know what can happen, it is all the more important. Peer pressure can do many things but if you don't give into it, you will be very proud of yourself and that is exactly how I feel. I believe in integrity even more now after being put to the test.

I believe in integrity.

One Saturday when I was thirteen, my family decided it was time to move Grandma to an adult care center. Feeble from persistent sickness, Gram barely had the strength to climb out of bed in the mornings. Dad knew it was time to gain 24-hour-a-day support for her.

We all piled into the car and headed to Gram's apartment. Eighty-one years of life's accumulated treasures awaited our agitated hands. Thank goodness Gram left with Dad for the day. Like fierce vultures, we pounced on our pillage.

One goal focused our efforts—clean out Gram's apartment. Peeling back layer by precious layer, I began my conquest in her guest room. With brutal evaluation, I easily categorized Gram's cherished belongings; to keep or to sell, that was the question.

Ten long hours of boring through Gram's possessions left me exhausted and disturbed. Distressing questions oppressed my mine. "Could all riches quickly be expelled in one day? What would Gram think if she knew—her purchased memories from travels afar, her esteemed heirlooms? What about her years spent caring for her valuables now soon to be sold at a garage sale? How must it feel to only own one plain suitcase of simple clothing at her new residence?

It was this turning point in my life when integrity deeply impressed itself upon my spirit. Integrity is undiminished honesty to oneself. Total freedom powered me when I realized I would passionately live in full truth without pursuing endless possessions. I felt abundant peace knowing my life would matter. I'd strive to be influential not impressive.

-Staff

Middle school is like the rain forest. Seeing the connection between the two may be king of confusion, but truthfully middle school is like the rain forest. The building is the actual land, and the people within are the animals. I'm not saying that the people here eat each other; no, that would be just wrong.

This being said, I believe in interdependence because we all depend on each other. I believe this for two reasons. One, I can't count the number of times I've needed my friend's help. I depend on them to help me. Two, all middle schoolers effect each other. I know, how cheesy does that sound? But it really is true.

When I was in 7th grade, P.E. was one of the mandatory classes to take. Everyone was assigned a small locker, given a combination, and was set free to go explore the locker. Unfortunately, I was never taught or told how to open a locker. Standing in the middle of the locker room, I watched everyone with mild curiosity as the small knot of panic tightened.

Needing to stop myself from having a full-blown panic attack, I looked at the paper the teacher had given me. Locker 400, with a combination easy enough to remember. I half-heartedly walked to my locker, noting I was beside two eighth grade girls who were sharing a locker.

Glancing down at my combination, I turned the lock one way and then another. Only to be slightly disappointed when the locker wouldn't budge. Trying again didn't bring any better news. Glaring at my locker and yelling at it from inside my head also did nothing.

The two eighth graders, that had been completely forgotten moments before, suddenly asked if I needed help. First, thinking it was a joke, I just stood there not sure how to reply. I had heard eighth graders were the bane of most seventh graders. After a moment of awkward silence, I realized it wasn't a joke. Nodding my head up and down and taking a small step back, I allowed the girls to help me.

Reading off the combination, and allowing them to show me what to do, I realized I needed them to help me. I depended on them to help me, not because they were the only one's that would help me, but because they were the only one's who offered. In the end the locker never did open, so I would put my stuff in a friend's locker. But the kindness those two eighth graders showed me, has made me realize it doesn't necessarily matter what happens, all that matters is who helps you get there and what you do with their help.

I believe middle school is like the rain forest, everything here depends on each other to learn and to survive, whether it be surviving middle school or surviving the jungle.

This I believe.

It was a time long, long, ago when I was maybe eight or nine years old; the fun, "absent-minded" years of my life--when you could sip a juice box and not look like a sissy. I had must moved in that year and had immediately bonded with my new neighbor, who was about my age. We would play games like, World War I, Aliens vs. Animals, and one game that I didn't fully understand, but it required a lot of screaming, jumping, running around, and dancing. Whenever I got hurt (which was often), my neighbor would get scared out of his mind and repeat, "Are you OK? Are you all right? How many fingers am I holding up?" It was funny how quickly he went from "King of the World," to a hospital nurse.

One day, we were playing on top of a huge muddy hill with sharp rocks sticking out of ponds below. (It is now that I would like to remind everyone that I was only eight or nine. So, Don't judge me!). I was pretending to be a Native American named Zacara, the rock collector. My neighbor was a Veteran named Jared, the hunter! "Jared" and I had finally reached the summit of what we now cal Mt. Mud, but the top was where the trouble began. I was standing there when the ground below my feet began to slide apart! Fortunately, I was flailing my arms, out of fear, and managed to grab hold of the peak. Then my neighbor sprung into action, got onto his knees and yelled, "Grab my hand!". This came across me as shocking because I had imagined that he would let me fall straight into the muddy water, ironically full of sharp objects. What I had imagined was wrong. I grabbed hold of his hand and he pulled me back onto my feet.

Interdependence

To this day he still rubs that in my face, but I am just happy he was there. That is why I believe I should live life, but be kind to others, they will be kind in return.

I believe that with interdependence, you can deal with anything life throws your, way. When I was five, one of the most difficult things to accept occurred; my grandpa died.

As my family and I pulled up to his driveway, cop cars and ambulances swarmed his property. Being so young, I automatically clenched my arms around my mom. I was filled with fear and panic. Then, climbing up the concrete steps to the door and opening it to see multiple relatives, tears like waterfalls from their eyes. It was a surreal moment.

I was then ushered out to the backyard, the very place I had so many memorable experiences, like collecting Easter eggs, while in the summer my family and I took delight in the pool. Spotting a blue tarp in the yard, we stumbled over. Two cops sluggishly lifted the tarp to reveal the peaceful face of my grandpa. My mom burst into tears, burying her face into my dad's shoulder, knowing that he was gone.

After that day, it wasn't the simplest of times for us, but the support we were able to provide each other made coping that much easier. Reliance on each other made us able to grow as a family unit. I believe in interdependence.

    I believe in interdependence because it helps you accomplish things that you would never be able to do by yourself. People all over the world work together to complete challenging tasks. Nearly all jobs in the world involve the employees working as a group to do their duties for their company and to finish the jobs they are supposed to do. The earlier in life that people learn about interdependence, the better off they will be.

    A time in my life when I began to understand interdependence was when I began to play sports when I was little. In the beginning, I always wanted to win by myself. I wanted to be the pitcher, make all the baskets and score all the goals.

    At first I was able to do this because the games weren't very competitive. As I got older, the other people got better. I soon learned that I couldn't win by myself. I had to work with my teammates to do this. I realized that it was best to let people do parts as a team where their strengths are used best. Everyone has things they are good at, which can help the team.

    I now understand that working as a team is much better than working alone. When people work together in a group, they and do much more challenging things than they could do by themselves.

    I believe in interdependence because it will help you to do things that you could never do by yourself.

I believe interdependence is everybody needing each other in different ways because nobody can do it on their own. I never knew I needed to count on someone or ever need that person's help. But, what I learned was everybody needs someone or something to lean on. We all need someone to lend us a helping hand or someone to be there when we are down.

Walking into science class, with a C grade gave me more stress than I could handle. I didn't want anyone's help. It was getting closer to the end of the trimester, and I knew I was running out of time. At one point, I knew I needed someone's help, so I turned to one of my classmates, also my friend, for help. The saying "two heads are better than one". I've always thought it wasn't true, but once I got help and saw my "C" slowly turn into a B, I realized that my brain and my friend's brain were better than one. Now I have been working really hard to earn an A and I know it's okay to ask for help because as I found out, the more I don't ask for help, the deeper I get into trouble.

Everything and everyone needs someone. In many ways we do need one another even when we don't know it. Sometimes we think we'll be fine by ourselves, but in the end, it's always good to have a friend. A person you can depend on and support.

I believe that when we depend on each other, life will be an easier task to complete, and to complete well. We have to learn to trust each other, be honest with each other. Being interdependent is what will bond us with our family and with friends. It helps resolve tension between countries and governments.

I learned to be interdependent with a good friend of mine. I remember there was a time when I had a few problems – unanswered questions. The two of us decided to meet up. The rendezvous place was the neighborhood Sharpies. There, sitting at a small table under a low hanging lamp, I took a leap of faith and decided to really trust the guy and tell him everything. I told him everything I was carrying with me for the past weeks.

He helped me. He told me how to resolve those issues I had. I knew he would be able to. However, what happened next was a surprise. When he was done answering my questions, he started telling me certain things. I wasn't expecting the guy to trust me like that. Because, in my mind at least, what he told me seemed like pretty big stuff.

That night at a restaurant, I learned what it was like to be interdependent; to trust, and to be trusted. And, it's true, after that day, it felt as if we got closer, as if I got to know him more.

When people learn to be truly interdependent; to truly rely and need other, that is when the world will be a better place. When people and countries take a step toward others and work together to learn to need each other; when people stop wasting money on destroying others, and start spending more on building relationships, that's when there will be true world peace. But, until then, there still will be distrust, hatred and war. People! Let's take a step to each other instead of separating steps. I pray God Almighty helps us become more interdependent. Because that is when people will truly love me, and I will truly love them.

I believe that encouragement can change the course of someone's life. I grew up one of three in a single parent family. For my siblings and I, this meant we got away with things we probably shouldn't have. Without much direction, I wandered through adolescence without much thought about the course I was on or where my life was going. It wasn't that I was on the wrong path, it was that I didn't even realize that there was a path because I had never considered my destination. This changed for me when I moved my sophomore year of high school. I entered a new school my junior year. I had a guidance counselor who started talking to me about the future and helped me plan what steps to take to attend a 4 year college with no money. She surrounded me with other students who had goals and a strong work ethic. She put me in AP classes, where I was challenged and had to work hard, instead of skating through. Because of her influence, I began to set goals and work hard. This was a big change for someone who was used to waiting for life to happen. I believe that her encouragement completely changed the course my life was on.

-Staff

I believe in the power of Family. I grew up in an average family of 5, one brother, one sister and me the oldest. We were fortunate to be raised into a household that had the same two parents. Mom the strong, gentle, kind matriarch, who has worked tirelessly all her life for the betterment of education. (all of which was without pay, much to the chagrin of my Father) Dad, who worked as a Portland State University professor for thirty-five years. My parents are married to this day. All of my memories as a child and moving onto adulthood are centered around this group of five that I refer to as family. A lot of my core beliefs, such as what is valuable, what is important, who comes first. come from this group. beliefs like: the power of education, reading for entertainment as well as for learning, and who is important in your life.

Not unique to my childhood and young adulthood were a host of wonderful people and fantastic learning opportunities. It was not just that I have had many people come through my life, but the kind of people that parents brought into our life. People who were colorful, like one dad's students we got to meet at a summer session down at the Oregon Institute of Marine Biology. Prince was truly a child of the sixties, his love for learning was ever present as he payed attention during one of my fathers many field trips out into the tidal flats of the Oregon Coast. Also ever present was his favorite hat a fuzzy toilet seat cover. These and many other examples told me that it is okay to find your own way. My path has yet to include a toilet seat cover, but it is nice to believe that that is an option. The influences and exposures that I experienced from being around my family is vast and varied, but I owe who I am to my family.

Family has many meanings to many people there is the legal definition, and the feelings and beliefs that one has. I have many people in my life that I count as bothers and sisters as much as my own blood relations. Even our son Jeffrey, who is adopted, could not be more our son. My wife we are legally married, and yet did we need that piece of paper to say we love each other and want to be together always. Shawna is a great source of strength and stability in my life. I owe much to these members of my family who are not blood relations. I can't imagine a life without Jeffrey. He was a gift from a person who made a choice to adopt as part of a plan that was going to better for her and her unborn child. This very legal and orchestrated bringing together of child and parents is very different from the feelings of family that we have for our son. Yet he is very much a part of who we are and Jeffrey has contributed much to my beliefs as to the strengths of family.

Friends who, like the sun, are always there. To witness and be a part of the thing called life. The friends you can count on, the ones I call brother and sister as often as my own siblings Tim and Rachel. Wife and son there, who give love and support. There are many things I believe in, but without my family and the strength I draw from them it is hard to say what I would be or believe.

-Staff

I have come to believe that with the help of friends and laughter, you can overcome any task.

I have a chronic ankle injury. The pain level increases and decreases as time goes on. Unfortunately, this will happen throughout the rest of my life.

This year has been the hardest for me. I have been to physical therapy, but the pain keeps reoccurring.

One day, one of my very best friends, Taylor, and I were sitting out of the dance class. She had a knee injury, and I had an ankle injury. We were both upset over our miserable injuries. She talked and I ate. Later, I talked and she ate. The process repeated, for what seemed like hours.

Eventually, I decided to break the cycle. I told her the most ridiculous joke I could think of (which I had found on a candy wrapper several days earlier). It was, "Why don't aliens put door bells on their space ships?"

She simply replied, "I have no idea," in an unenthusiastic tone.

I addressed her answer in a mocking way and put on a false smile, "Because they wanted to win the NO-BELL prize!"

Her only response was laughter. Pure laughter! She couldn't stop laughing. As her giggles reached me, I felt a feeling stir within me. It was happiness. It had been a very long time since I had been overcome with pure joy, due to my unfortunate injury. Later, I started to laugh with her. I laughed until my stomach hurt and my cheeks became numb. Taylor continued to laugh. Then, I just watched as

Laughter

the happy emotions continued to take over her. Then, I laughed with her some more!

In the midst of all the laughter, I realized something. I was no longer upset over that "miserable" injury. Neither was Taylor. My ankle injury had just gone from an inconvenience to an opportunity. An opportunity to grow my bond with Victoria among other people. From that point on, I realized that no matter what, I could depend on Taylor and her gorgeous giggles to help me feel better.

For many years, I believed that some situations were unsolvable. After that day with Taylor, I learned that there is always something or someone to hold you back. But, there is always something or someone that will pull you past that set-back. In this case, it was my wonderful friend Victoria and laughter! In short, I always remember that a little laughter and a friend can help any situation.

I believe that laughter can change the world. Two years ago my grandma died. I was 10 years old when it happened.

My mom and her five brothers met at my grandma's old white house after the funeral. My 30 year old cousin had set up a slide show of pictures of my grandma when she was alive. The pictures showed many memories: camping at Dworshak Reservoir, Christmas Eve at her house, the time she caught a fish that was almost as tall as she was. It became very uncomfortable as my whole family started to cry. A few more pictures showed up on the screen when suddenly there was a picture of my 3 year old cousin crawling on my grandma's back at her birthday party. All of my sad family members began to laugh. What was a morbid atmosphere turned into a happy one as we all cracked up. The pictures kept changing, but we kept laughing. This small reminder of the joy that our deceased family member brought us acted as a trigger to wipe away the memories of my dead grandma and replace them with memories of the alive one.

If laughter can change a sad group of people to a happy group, then laughter can change happy people into happier people. This is why I think laughter can change the world.

I believe that people should laugh more. I also believe that people should be accepted by others and accepting to others. I can remember a time when it made me feel comfortable in school. It was sometime around the time I had just started Happy Valley Middle. I didn't know anyone except for my friends Julia and Erica. But they were seventh graders. Then, when I got to 3rd period language arts and I met Andrew, Zach, and Tyler. We were making popsicle sticks with our names on them. I was passing them out and when I got to the table with Andrew, Zach and Tyler, one of them asked my name. I told them "Asia". They didn't believe me at first. When Andrew was collecting the sticks, he read mine and said "Wow your name really is Asia." From that day forward we've been friends. I still laugh about that day too.

Laughing at them for not believing me made me feel happy and excited that I had made some new friends one of my first few days of school.

I can also remember the time I felt accepted. It was around the same time when I met Tyler, Zach and Andrew. I was in 5th period social studies. I was sitting at a table with Toria, M'kaila, Michelle, and Alex. I used to be afraid of them. I thought that they were mean, snobby girls, so I stayed quiet and didn't look at them at all. But one day Toria looked at me and said "Girl you gotta loosen up a little!" And we have been friends since that day. I'm glad that I got to know them. They weren't mean or snobby at all. They were really nice. I felt accepted that day. I am so glad that I went through these experiences.

Now I know how hard it is for new students. My memories of laughter and acceptance are mostly the main reasons why I believe in laughing more and being accepted or being accepting to others. Even though these students will not read my essay I want them and everyone to know that I appreciate how they treated me when I first moved to Oregon from Tennessee.

This I believe.

I believe that laughter can brighten up any ones day, even at the worst of times.

I sat down on the couch to watch some TV, but before I turned it on, I glanced over at my mom, to see her crying. I couldn't ask her why or what was wrong because she was on the phone. I didn't know who she was talking to or what it was about, all I knew was it was sad. Finally she hung up, and I was able to ask " Who was that?"

"That was Aunt Martha…Uncle Doug has passed away," Mom replied, in a depressed voice. It became so clear. The sadness hit me, and I could feel the tears flow down my face.

A few months earlier doctors found a tumor on his brain. Since then his symptoms had drastically increased. The tumor grew faster than we all expected. It was pretty obvious he was going to die; I just didn't expect it to be that soon.

His memorial was a few weeks after he passed away. It was held at a college, in the drama room. That day was very sad, although it did feel good to see my mom's side of the family again.

We watched a slide show of pictures that showed funny and happy moments with Uncle Doug. At the end of the memorial, we told stories about him, most of them were funny. Every so often there were stories that were heart warming and touching.

When people told the funny stories, it was like the whole room lit up, like it wasn't a memorial service any more. After the laughter ended, we went back to sadness, back to reality, back to the memorial.

At the end of the memorial we were actually kind of happy. We were very sad, but not as sad as we were before we arrived. I'm actually kind of glad we went (not like there was a choice), but it wasn't as sad as I thought it would be.

I believe that laughter can brighten up anyone's day, even at the worst of times.

This I believe.

I believe that laughter is like an instant vacation. Laughter for me is a daily process. If laughter were a person we would be best friends. This reminds me of a time when I was at a summer camp. On the first day I met a boy named Ryan. He had a disorder called Autism. As the days went by Ryan and I became closer and closer. Ryan was a boy that I cared dearly about; he used to say the funniest things.

What was so special about him is that he used to make me laugh and I love to laugh. There was something special about when we laughed. I forgot everything around me and I didn't even remember he had a disorder, and that reminds me of vacation.

I forget about everything when I go on vacation and just have a good time. The one thing that I realized, besides laughing with anyone is fun, is that I want to become a special ed. teacher. I want to help kids like Ryan who can learn but usually at a slower pace. Just one summer with Jake changed my whole perspective of life and that was a summer I will never forget. Laughter is like an instant vacation.

This I believe.

I believe in laughing until your sides hurt, even at the most random things. I also believe that if there are one hundred reasons to cry, there are one hundred and one reasons to laugh. An example of this was when my friend and I were at my house, doing homework….

It started one fine spring day. My friend Bob-their name really isn't Bob, but I'm going to call them that for this story-and I were finishing our homework in my mom's sewing room. I did most of my homework in class, so I finished before Bob. I started reading one of my favorite books, "Where the Sidewalk Ends," by Shel Silverstein. While reading, I stumbled upon a poem called, "Me too". It wasn't really funny, but for me it was just hilarious. I started cracking up so hard, and Bob just sat there staring at me. I couldn't stop laughing, so I just handed Bob the book. And as soon as he finished reading it he started laughing as hard as I was. We couldn't stop laughing, and it was one of the best days of my life.

I believe laughter is powerful, ever since I was a baby people have been able to make me laugh. No matter how old, how big, how small or how sad you are, there is always someone out there that can make you laugh. Laughter turns frowns upside down.

I believe laughter whispers to your soul, it's the key to happiness. I was once told that laughing is healthy. I believe with all my heart that laughter improves your heart, mind, and soul.

Depression is bad right? So why not laugh more, cherish and keep it for later? I believe that laughter is the key to happiness.

Without laughter people would be dull, the world would be lifeless and there wouldn't be true happiness. Your laugh is unique, it's yours and only yours, God gave it to you, so use it. Laughter is a gift and it makes you....you.

Laughter can make a sad person happy, laughter can make you cry, laughter can make your stomach hurt and laughter can brighten anyone's day. Laughter is magical, it has this power that comes from deep inside of you and pulls the stress away.

I Believe Laughter Is Powerful.

I believe in laughter being the best medicine. Laughter has given me relief in times of stress and in times of pain. One day comes to mind when laughing felt particularly therapeutic and totally unexpected. Six year ago, I received a phone call that my brother-in-law had died. Mike was a wonderful man. A man so full of life that it just couldn't be true. He had been a part of my life for 32 years. Making others laugh was a gift of his. Often at family gatherings, Mike would start in on the jokes and was relentless with the puns. Everyone would boo him with a smile on their face and a giggle in their throat, me included. I always appreciated the fact that I could count on him to make me laugh. So, the day of his funeral was the most heart-wrenching day that I have ever encountered. The tears flowed, and my heart felt its heaviest. At the end of this long, sad day, the family gathered at his gravesite and the strangest thing happened. Puns started rattling off everyone's tongues. How it started or who started it is a mystery. Everyone was laughing. It was a sight, thirty people laughing in a cemetery. Reflecting on that day, I smile and feel that laughter healed my heart.

Quoting the poet E.E. Cummings, I too believe, "The most wasted of all days is one without laughter."

-Staff

    I believe in the power of people. Bringing people together as a family brings out the light from love to help us have a bright future. Together, not as a community, but as a family we walk through many doors, and many times we are wrong, but as long as we are together we will outstand the rocks that life throws at us. I believe that people are amazing, no one is bad. I believe that we can make the world a better place by being together, helping, loving, and living our lives to fulfill our dreams. Together we will grow into one big planet filled with love, peace, and family. I believe we are one.

When I was 7 years old, I wanted a puppy. So my mom and dad took me to the pound to adopt one. As I was walking around I saw all of these little jumpy dogs. But when I turned around, there was this helpless little puppy just lying there. I told my parents that I wanted that puppy. So we took the puppy home, and we named him Fuzzy. It was part Lhasa Apso and part Shitzo. Fuzzy made a great addition to our family. Everybody loves him. Fuzzy is the best thing that has happened in my life. He has made a huge impact on my family (in a good way!). I believe that everyone, everything, needs love.

Love is one of the strongest things in the world! But you may not realize that you have it until it's gone or almost gone.

My family was sitting outside on the deck watching our dog Lucky run around and be silly. My dad was sitting out there very quietly in a lawn chair. I could tell he wanted to say something and I was right.

"I think we are going to have to get rid of Lucky" he said. My mom and me stared at him like what are you talking about. "He's getting to be too much work and I don't think I can handle it anymore." My mom and I knew that he was on this medicine that makes him that way because he has cancer.

"Are you kidding me?!?!" my mom finally said. I couldn't sit there anymore. I ran to my room to cry.

My dad came into my room saying, "I know that was a shock to you but I thought about it and we don't have to get rid of him. I realize how much you LOVE him and I would never want to take that away."

I have never realized I loved something that much until the moment of truth hit me.

Love & Kindness

I remember making sandwiches for homeless teenagers when I was eleven and twelve. It happened at all of our families' houses; we traded off time with each other. It wasn't just a couple of people who helped, it was my whole family. We would make the sandwiches, have dinner and have a great time. After all the sandwiches were done we would put them in a paper bag with some pretzels and a small candy bar. When they were all in the bag we would put them into a large bucket. After that day when we had about 100 sandwiches we would take them to a homeless teenager shelter. When we got there we unloaded the big bucket and took it upstairs to a lady in the kitchen part of the shelter. We always did this, even though the place changed. Our whole family would get together the first Sunday of every month.

Doing this always made me feel good. Making sandwiches being with family and taking the sandwiches to the shelter. Before we started doing this good deed all I did was sympathize about the homeless. Now that I have done this I can proudly say I have empathized. By doing this I also made the homeless feel good even though they don't have a home. I believe that if you can help yourself you can help anyone else.

I believe in faith. Being a Christian is an important part of my life. When I was 3 or 4 years old I asked my dad what the real reason I went to church was. It didn't take long for me to really understand. I asked why I needed a relationship with God and he told me all of the stuff. I asked how I can grow with God and he replied with me going to church. I now am strong and have courage in my faith. Everyday, because of my faith, I think at school about everything that would help me in my faith. I think of helping others, respecting others, being nice to others, doing stuff that makes me glad I did them. I treat others the way I want to be treated. I look back on that day, going from knowing nothing important to me other than friends and family, to being good towards my faith. I believe that my religion/faith makes me a stronger, better, nicer, more trustworthy and giving person.

Faith never fails. I believe in faith. When have words been able to describe something. Having and believing in faith means the world to me. People can't live without certain things. What's a teacher without students. Faith is what completes me. Faith is the secret to trust, loyalty and believing. Believing that you can do what ever you put your mind. Having hope that everything will turn out the way it's supposed to. Living day by day with your head held up high, taking steps with confidence and in your mind with one word "faith". Faith is the closest thing to magic. It's like having a want and making all your dreams, hopes, and wishes true. Faith isn't a thing or word, it's a reality. It's something that will never let you down. Never let the odds keep you from what you were meant to do. Follow your heart. Dream as if you'll live forever. Faith never fails!

Last year in 6th grade there was a kid in my class named Jordan. Although Jordan was both nice and smart, he still had problems at school and at home. At school everyone picked on him while at home he had no dad.

Throughout the school year kids continued to pick on Jordan. Even though Jordan got angry and mad, he always forgave the people that were constantly hurting him over and over. At times, I wondered why he forgave them, but I could never find the answer.

Near the middle of the school year, Jordan had to move to a different state. When he didn't show up to class, our teacher told us that Jordan had been crying because he loved his school and his community. It was then that I found the answer. Jordan forgave us because he was a good person that cared about other people, and not just himself. I couldn't believe that I hadn't seen it sooner. It should have been a really easy thing to see because Jordan always helped people with school work and showed concern when someone got hurt. Even if the person that got hurt was the bully that picked on him the day before.

Witnessing this has made me believe in kindness and respect. Since the day Jordan left, I have tried to show kindness and respect to everyone I meet because everyone is a human, and they all have feelings.

Love & Kindness

I have tried to show kindness and respect to everyone I meet because everyone is a human, and they all have feelings. When you're feeling down or sad, one smile from someone else can make you feel better. It reminds you that there's always people out there to help you in times of sadness. That's how I felt when Briana smiled at me when I was feeling down.

I came to school feeling down because earlier that day at home, my mom told me that my family would be moving soon. I didn't want to leave all my friends. I was sitting in my seat, staring at the wood on my desk, when I just looked up for no reason. Briana was at her desk doing her math. She saw me looking at her with my sad eyes. And she smiled at me.

That smile reminded me that life isn't always the way you wish it was. That good and bad things happen. No matter where you go, there will always be someone to help you. I believe that one smile can brighten up anyone's day. This is what I believe.

I believe in kindness. I believe in going outside your box to share with and be nice to others. When I was in 4th grade, my family and I lived in Costa Rica for a month. One native family was kind enough to let us stay in their home for our duration there. However, they did not simply stop at this. They would let us eat meals with them, we would go to the beaches together, and they taught us a lot about their culture.

At that time, my whole family could speak Spanish reasonably well, so their family and mine talked a lot and shared our stories. I have almost never met such a kind group of people, and one that was so willing to share. One teenager, nicknamed "Nacho," was always willing to entertain my siblings and I.

He showed us how to catch lizards and hermit crabs, how to climb trees to pick fruit, and much more. I will always remember the day we all took turns trying to get avocados out of trees with his slingshot.

That family really taught me to share what I have, and to always try to be nice to others. The first day we arrived, 10-year-old Alex immediately ran up to us and asked if we wanted to play soccer or Frisbee with him. You should always be kind to people, even those that you barely know. This I believe.

When I was in the 2nd grade we had a secret santa party. Everyone was super excited to see when their gift was. To start the whole thing, everyone got their gift they had purchased and got into a circle. The rules to the game were as soon as you heard a certain word from the book the teacher was reading us, we would have to stop passing around the gifts, and by the end of the story whatever gift you had in your hands was yours. As our teacher, Mrs. Whitecotton, started reading people would shake the gifts to see if they could guess what was in it. It was almost the end of the book and people started passing them around like hot potatoes. When the story was finished everyone was tearing the wrapping paper off and when I opened mine, I was so happy. I got a board game, and a special needs boys, named David, who has been in my class forever, got those learning flashcards. He was so disappointed. I felt really bad because he was going to have no use for them and that was his present. I took another look at my present and then his and got up, walked over to him and asked if he would like to switch presents with me. His face lit up and he immediately grabbed the present without thinking and saying thank you to me. But the look on his face was enough for me. I didn't need a thank you. That moment and type of experience in my life has a lot to do with who I am today. I believe in sharing with others and being kind.

I believe love gets us through each and every day.

My mom carefully wrapped the pearl necklace around my neck. She hooked it in the back and let it fall loose. I looked at myself in the mirror. Standing there, my hair curled and a black dressed smoothed against my sides, my cheeks swirled into a rosy red color. It was one of the first times I had ever gotten ready to attend a funeral.

She was never extremely close to me, my grandmother. But when the day came and she was no longer there to talk to me on the phone for hours, hug me, never letting go, and laugh her trademark laugh, I realized how much she meant to me. My grandmother was always there to help me through my childhood, make me laugh, and teach me valuable lessons in life.

As I sat there on the wooden pew, hands folded in my lap and eyes glancing in every which way, I wondered whether she was looking down on my sister and me. I glanced towards my great aunt and she smiled tenderly. In that moment, I became aware that I wasn't alone. Everyone in the entire church missed my grandma. All of us were there to support one another and love each other through that tough time. And now I recognize that even though my grandma has passed, the love we had from her and for her will never change. The love will not be lost.

We let the butterflies free. Unleashing them from within their trapped boxes, the butterflies fluttered gracefully into the purple of the sky. I, and the rest of the people from the memorial, watched them disappear into the world stretched beyond. It was then when I realized love is

Love & Kindness

like a butterfly. Love is the fragile wings that carry us to any destination and keep up moving, even through the toughest journeys. I believe love gets us through each and every day.

A chapter in my life that has changed my way of thinking not only in my mind, but also in my heart, is when my parents got divorced. I was only five years old when it happened. As a young child, I never worried about my parents splitting up. The thought had never crossed my mind. I do, however, remember the event like it was last night. My brother and I were sitting at the table with our mom and dad eating dinner. Our big Disney World vacation was coming up very soon. It was my first time going and it was all I could think about. As I took a bite of my meal, my parents announced they had something to tell my brother and me. I wasn't worried it was going to be anything bad.

"Your mother and I are getting a divorce," my dad said in a tone I hadn't heard him use before. It sounded sort of depressing and mad.

At the time I didn't even know what the word divorce meant. The only question I could manage to pop out of my mouth was, "Are we still going to Disney World?"

"Yes," my mom said as though she had something more important on her mind, which she definitely did.

Now that I understand what the word divorce means, I kind of think of it as going to the store to buy eggs, only when you get home you realize they're rotten and then decide to return them for your money back.

A few years ago, after my parents became divorced, a feeling came upon me that brought up great sadness. My dad told my brother and I that he felt he had neglected us and wanted to spend more time with us. Then we got into counseling, which I guess helped, but I hated sharing my feelings with a man I barely knew, while my dad was just sitting there staring at me, listening to my every word.

When I think about it, I guess the way my parents divorce affected me and the way it still does is sort of like yin and yang; if I never experienced sad I wouldn't know what that feeling was. In some ways, that would be considered a good thing. But then I wouldn't have an emotion that connects me in a way to every other human and creature on the planet.

Moments like these that have happened in my life remind me that loving and spending time with my family is my number one priority in life. Because I never know how long I will have them around. With that in mind, I know I must make every moment count.

I believe in doing good things, even if no one is watching. Growing up in a close, protective family, I was given everything I wanted: I got to travel the world, sail on first-class cruise ships, buy only name-brand clothing. I never for once actually decided to give my clothes away to the poor or donate my unused toys to the toy drives. I never even bothered to make a difference in my own community. I was simply just selfish and spoiled. However, I wanted to change. I wanted to finally break my streak of conceited acts and do something about it. And actually, I did.

It all started on a crisp October morning. Me, my sister, and a few other friends of mine were sitting in my leadership teacher's van outside of Happy Valley Middle School. A few days ago, I decided to join my classmates on a fieldtrip to downtown Portland. Although I expected to go to shopping malls and eat at some really sophisticated and fancy cafes, my leadership teacher, Mrs. Lute, had different plans; we were going to give out food to marathon runners. "This is a great way to serve our community," she said. So we were supposed to go to downtown Portland to give out food? That was no way of spending a Sunday. But before I was going to bail out, I said to myself, "Come on Jennifer. Let's do this. It will be fun. It will be fun...."

I was tired. And groggy. But hey, we finally reached our destination of downtown Portland! After parking on the side of a road, everyone (including me) piled out of the van and onto the sidewalk. "Ok everyone," Mrs. Lute commanded. "I want all of you to put on these t-shirts." She pulled out a small stack of neatly folded white

Love & Kindness

t-shirts and handed them out. As I received mine, I carefully observed it. The garment had a little stick-figure in the middle in a running position; above it was in all caps, VOLUNTEER. "How embarrassing," I mumbled to myself. But once I got my shirt on, Mrs. Lute hollered, "Let's go!"

Following everyone down the sidewalk, I did a quick mental check: Impatient, irritated, and tired? Yes. Having the time of my life? No. "Only a few more minutes of walking kids," Mrs. Lute yelled. "Don't worry! The fun will come later." After what seemed like forever, we arrived at our area. Tables and more tables piled high with food surrounded the entire road where the runners were supposed to enter after finishing. Candy, cookies, chips and milkshakes; I thought the food was for us. However, my daydreaming soon got cut short. "Ok girls," Mrs. Lute said. Me, my twin sister Julie, and my friend Melissa all turned toward her. "I want you three to go to that station over there." She pointed to a long table. "And one more thing. When you're finished handing out candy, you can have some of it if you like." Nodding in agreement, we darted across the street, avoiding getting run over by some of the marathoners. However, once we reached our station, I totally forgot that this was a community service project.

Candy, Hershey bars, KitKats, M&Ms; they were everywhere. Standing behind the table, we were assigned to give the sweets to the runners and say "Congratulations" to every one of them. Although I thought that saying "Congratulations" a hundred times would be pretty tiring for my mouth, I supposed being given some candy in return for my hard work would be worth it, too. After waiting a few minutes, I finally got my first runner. She was a short, brown-haired girl who seemed to be in her mid 20's. "Congratulations," I said in my sweetest voice. "That

Love & Kindness

must've been a tough 26 miles." "Oh yes," she sighs. I could obviously tell she was exhausted.

"Would you like some candy?"

"Of course! Let me think….how about Almond Joy. I love those."

"Ok, here you go." I handed her two Almond Joys and she gratefully takes them.

"It's so great that you would spend your time helping people like this. Thank you so much," she says. I wave at her, and as she's leaving, she waves back and takes a bite of her candy. Smiling, I look up at the blue sky. "What a feeling," I whisper to myself. All my life I have felt happy, sad, mad, glad, but I have never felt this way before. I never thought that such a little thing like giving someone candy can make their day. I truly believe that we should do good things; it simply makes our world go round.

I believe in kindness. My story happened a long time ago, but I remember it clearly. I was in 8th grade. I had lots of friends because I lived in the same town my whole life and because there were only a hundred people in my whole grade, everybody knew everybody.

One day, we had free time at school and the teacher let us go outside. I was with some other people hanging out by the side of the school. A girl who had only been at our school for about two weeks was sitting on the steps. One of my friends ordered me to go call the new girl a name and emphasized "to her face." I was petrified and didn't want to become an outcast. I didn't want to do it. I didn't think I was a mean person and she seemed nice. Before I knew it, I had blurted out, "ok," and started walking toward her. The group was watching.

She looked up when I got close to her and I just blurted out, "How's it goin'? She said, "pretty good," and we ended up hitting it off and talking for a minute or two. She became one of my best friends. I always wondered what would have happened if I had done what my "friend" told me to do. It reminded me to always do what I think is right even if other people encourage me to do something else.

I believe in kindness, and in forgiveness. My "friend" made a mistake and the consequence was missing out on a really great friendship. Everybody makes mistakes and part of kindness is learning from those mistakes and moving forward.

-Staff

I believe in the hugging. This morning while getting ready for work I smashed my daughter's fingers in the bathroom door. My oldest daughter, Madelyn, needed to use the bathroom and my youngest daughter, Maya, wouldn't move as she was sitting on the toilet blowing her nose. As arguments between my daughters sometimes go, I had to intervene. Seeing my oldest girl as I opened the bathroom door, I quickly shut it to give her privacy, not noticing my little pip squeak hiding behind the door with her fingers in the jam. The pain to her fingers was intense and she cried in uncontrollable sobs. I held her, reassuring her that it was going to feel better and still she cried. Eventually the tears stopped and she lay in my arms holding on.

Growing up as a child in a divorced family, my sister and I lived with a mom that took on all roles to make our world work for us. As part of that she was the go-to person that helped meet our emotional needs. Hugging and saying that she loves you is part of who she is as a person and a parent. The missing link in all of this is that I didn't have a male role model that demonstrated those qualities. How were boys and men suppose to act? Having a father that I saw every other weekend and who was not an emotional or touchy person, did not provide me with the answer. As I got older I promised myself that when I had kids I would be the kind of father to hold and hug them almost to a fault.

That's how I start, and that's how I end.

-Staff

Our children need our love the most when they are the least lovable. It's easy to love the child who brings a bunch of flowers or always cleans their room, but it's harder to love the child who talks back and argues. And, it's the same with students. It's easy to love the student who turns in all their work on time, answers politely, and demonstrates respect. Our challenge is to love (and teach) that student who resists, or declines, to take part in his or her own education. Because I believe that the difficult student isn't really saying "I don't care about paragraphs", I believe that student is really saying "I need to know if anyone cares about me". And until that student "feels the love", they won't be good learners. So, I believe that our children need our love the most when they are the least lovable.

-Staff

colors
character dream
believe
challenges
different
encouragement
Failing destination
failing enough everyone's
fail **failure** final
give
fullest feelings
heart **goal** helps
jobs **hard** good keep
hope
makes mistakes living
learn perfect Mistakes
Perseverance People
life Never-give-up lot

PERSEVERANCE

practice perseverance reason
school persistence
sports Thoughts reveals
trying
trudging **work** tools
unless

It was fourth period and I was in orchestra, getting ready for the second play test. The students in my class were talking about how nervous they were and betting on who was going to have the highest score. I tuned out their conversations, knowing it has nothing to do with me and that I would not land a bet for competition. The outcomes are clear-you either win victorious or lose disappointed. My main goal was to get a higher score than last time which I got a ninety-three plus, leaving me in the middle of the second violin section.

Two people volunteered to go and both got a reasonable score. My palms started to sweat as I raised my hand to go third. My orchestra teacher nodded an approval and scribbled my name in her notebook. I changed to playing position and played the song memorized with determination. After hearing my play test, the teacher announced my score. I got a ninety-five plus, the highest score any seventh grade orchestra player has ever gotten. I was completely shocked and at the same time, proud of myself.

That one experience made me come to a belief. It's not about competing with others that matters, but competing with yourself. I take my focus into becoming a better violinist than the best violinist. Now, whenever there is a play test, I don't strive for first chair. All I care about is beating myself, which happens successfully all the time.

I believe no matter how smart you are, you can always learn more. I believe that statement because everybody learns new things each day. I have continuously learned new things as I have gotten older. Now, I'm in seventh grade and I know a lot more things than I knew in kindergarden. Getting to learn new things is important to me because it helps you later on in life. I believe no matter how smart you are anyone can always learn more.

"Just keep swimming. Just keep swimming...", I play the familiar musical quote from Disney's "Finding Nemo" in my head, yet stop a foot from the wall. Painting, I look up at the almost stranger who shakes her head in defeat.

This is my third attempt at swimming. I had gone to three different coaches, in hopes that they could teach me the basics. So I would know if swimming was for me. I couldn't even swim a single lap correctly? Perhaps I was meant to play another sport. Then I realized a belief that helped change my mind. I believe that the human mind is capable of anything. A sport, I would argue, is 70% mental, 30% physical, the latter perhaps an even smaller fraction.

So, I would try again. My father, a very strong supporter of me and my success, suggested that I try going to a professional coach. Maybe that would do the trick. Off we went, in pursuit of the coach who could give the final approval/disapproval, whatever awaited me. We found many professional coaches in the area, and settled for one who seemed to know what they were doing. My stomach was in knots after the previous failures but I was willing to try again.

After a thirty-minute session, I emerged out of the water victorious. Not only had I swam a half-decent lap. I had also felt a real connection with the sport. Following this, my swimming "career" only went up hill. I joined a noncompetitive team and when I excelled there, joined one of Oregon's top competitive swim teams.

Perseverance

It was difficult, and at times I wanted to give up but I would always think of the possibility of swimming becoming something to me. Lo and behold it has. The human mind is truly capable of anything: This I believe.

I believe that working hard is important, so work you're hardest at everything and you will get rewarded. I chose this belief statement because in this story, that is exactly what happened.

It was around 8:15 a.m. on a cloudy Saturday morning. My dad and I were driving to my game on the highway. When we got to Rosemont Middle School in West Linn, my dad was telling me I had to work hard and have energy because the last game wasn't very good. The coach was looking for people with energy. The game was intense. My team jumped off to a huge lead. I would describe the game with words like: drama, athleticism, sweat, support, and working hard.

In the second half we let them come back and they almost won. We held them to six points behind us. We won and we were glad. I found out that I had scored 18 points which is a career high for me. I was proud of my hard work and know it paid off in the most important game of the year. That game has taught me this belief: Working hard is important, so work your hardest at everything and you will get rewarded.

    I believe in persistence even if your nerves tell you otherwise. This can go for a lot of different things but for me, this is about dancing. I got on stage in front of my whole studio, many other studios, and most importantly the cameras. I was so close to getting a scholarship for $1,000 but unfortunately I forgot the steps on stage. I knew that some people were thinking why did they pick this girl when she doesn't even know the moves? This thought was battling my other thought of it is going to be ok. The beginning and end of the dance was perfect. This was the most embarrassing moment of my life. For days I thought I was never going to win the $1,000. Then I thought, I am a great dancer, and this isn't the end of the world. There are other auditions and chances. You just have to want them enough for them to come to you. I wanted this more than you could ever know. I believe persistence is the key to what you want, and your nerves are just another bump in the road.

    I believe dreams don't come true on their own, you have to work to make them. Ever since I was in T-ball, I dreamed of hitting a home run one day. As the years went by, I began thinking that I would never be able to because I had so many flaws with my hitting. For a portion of softball season, I struck out for swinging too early, and watching the ball zoom past me. I was sick and tired of striking out and being the underdog! I practiced and began going to the batting cages every weekend. My hard work paid off and I moved up to being first to bat every game. Even though I was good at batting, I still couldn't get the power to hit a home run.

    The next season of softball I tried out for the team I am normally always on. The coaches were looking at everyone's batting skill to see if they were good enough. I was the first to go and the pitcher I was hitting off of was the best and fastest pitcher in our age group. As the ball came at me, I was confident I would hit it as far as I could. I was right. I didn't only hit it far, I got a home run! Even though it was in practice, it was good enough for me.

    All of my hard work paid off and I realized that dreams do come true, but in order to make them, you have to work hard at it. I learned to never give up on my dreams. To this day I feel more confident in my abilities and I continue to push myself so that I can be the best I can be. I learned a lot about myself and what it takes to be good at something. This same reasoning can be used in many other areas in my life such as school, other sports, and when I eventually get a job.

    I believe in perseverance. People fail a lot, but some keep trying and trying, trudging to their final destination. Once you reach your goal, you know it was worth the fight. I fight for my presence. I persevere. Competitions get the worst out of me. I blubbered like a child when I lost a school dance competition. In the competition, people were cheering me and my partner on. We tried our best for all the songs, and in the end, our practice was wasted. My partner left for the rest of the activity day, and I was left walking towards the locker room, heart broken. The year after I tried again, but I left with another frog in my throat. I still have plenty more years to do something noticeable. Maybe my time in the limelight won't be from dancing but I'll try and try to make myself known. I simply believe in perseverance.

    I believe that things happen for a reason. I was four when my dad died. He died of a heart attack. This is the event that I am describing. He died in Texas ten years ago when I was in Oregon. My family were the people involved. Acceptance, death, health, age and family come to mind when I think about this. When I think back on this day, it makes me feel sad and what could have been. I would want to tell people that before this event I thought that this would never happen to my family. Now I know that everyday I should appreciate the people that I have in my life because they could be gone before I know it. Some values that were important to me back then were memories that I had with my dad before he died. Some values that are important to me now are memories, family and friends. I always wondered what would have happened if he was still alive, but that will never happen. I have learned to accept it but I do miss him a lot and think of what would have been. This I believe.

I have always wondered what life would be like if every person had a negative attitude. I image that if every person on the earth were to always sulk and mope about, the world in which we live in would be a ghastly and terrible place. Learning how to swim, is how I stumbled upon this important epiphany.

It all started during summer vacation while I was an awkward, timid, fifth grader. My grandpa had just signed up my brother and I for Level A swimming lessons at the North Clackamas Aquatic Park. When I entered the building for swimming lessons, the odor of human sweat and chlorine filled my aching lungs. There were so may people! If I moved three inches from front to back, and left to right, I would have immediately bumped into a wet body.

Of course, seeing all those people only made me regret coming to take swimming lessons all the while more! They would all see me go into the shallow end of the pool, with a bunch of four and six year olds, learning how to float and "glide". Nevertheless, I reluctantly strode into the calm, tranquil water, feeling mortified, nervous, anxious, and vehement. Although I was filled with sudden outburst of different emotions, the swimming instructors were very patient and sweet towards me. By the end of the lesson I wasn't feeling half bad. In fact, I was exuberant and completely engulfed in bliss. I was so proud of myself for surviving my first swimming lesson.

Accordingly, I took more and more swimming lessons to become a stronger swimmer. Finally, when the summer came to an end, I had already learned how to swim efficiently and powerfully. Now that I look back on that summer, I think that it was dumb of me to think that it would be impossible for me to learn how to swim. Especially because the words impossible itself say that "I'm possible". Learning how to swim is how I realized that if I had a positive and focused attitude, I could achieve events that occurred in my life. I believe life with an optimistic and determined attitude is the only way we should live. This I believe.

Tonight my mom and I argued. I crushed her, brought her down. I didn't think about what I was doing, not thinking about how my actions didn't only reflect on me, but I let it continue until the consequences bore down on me like a wave, pulling me under and drowning me in their salty weight.

Apologizing over and over doesn't help. It's too late for that. I either have to change soon or lose one of the most precious things I have.

I was walking with my head held too high. Sometimes the most valuable things can be found if you just stop to look for them. It's as if I was walking along a street on a warm summer day, not paying attention to anyone or anything but me. Deciding to look down, I see that in my path I have let destruction be in every footstep. I have let my sadness leak into the ground. Being so careless, thoughtless, I had stomped on and ignore the beauty of the earth. The ground wept, the flowers keeled over, bent out of shape. The consequences of my actions swirled around me.

I did exactly that to my mom. I stepped on that beautiful love she has for me, the love I have been taking for granted.

You can replant the flowers, you can grow them bigger, but they'll never be the same ones you had before. Even after the pain has healed, there is still a trace of what happened, all that pain and sadness.

I know that my mom and I will make up, we will laugh, cry, and hug many more times. We will also argue and get angry and sad. But happiness leaves a mark, too.

Happiness is when you replant those flowers and see them flourish and thrive. They aren't the same, but it's not like you can't ever find joy again.

Now I will look where I tread, I will be careful as to what kind of trail I leave: one of destruction or one of new growth, joy and hope. I believe that tomorrow will bring joy that will help us get past the pain and sadness. I believe that while our hearts will still bear scars in places they have been hurt, they can still be mended. A heart that has been broken holds on tighter to what's important.

I believe that my mistakes will make me more loving, hopeful, joyous, stronger, gentler and kinder than I would have been if I hadn't made them.

I believe that if you truly want something, work hard at it and keep on trying, you can make it happen. This way of thinking has definitely helped me with my confidence and positive outlook. I have tried out for many plays, competitions, etc., and I have only made less than half. I have noticed the more I want something and the harder I work at it, the more likely I am to succeed. There are times in my life when I wished that I would have followed this perspective. For example, a year ago I was in this Christmas show. There was a tryout for a gospel solo. I was really the only one in the choir that had that kind of voice, so I thought I had it in the bag. I didn't even practice it because I didn't feel the need. But I was shocked to hear the other girls sounding really, really good! So I didn't get the solo, but I bet if I had followed my new rule like the chosen girl had, I could have gotten it. Now I'm not saying I was guaranteed, but definitely more likely than how lazy and indulgent I had acted. So now for everything I do I try to put 100% out. If you truly want something, work hard at it and keep on trying. You can make it happen.

"I believe that perseverance and encouragement will get you through any situation."

A few years ago my mom was having problems with her car. It turns out that the engine was overheating after every few miles it was driven. My mother and I didn't know much about cars so to avoid this problem we would cool the engine down with water every few miles. It took about a month to get all the money to fix the car. When we got all the money we got a few gallons of water and headed toward a cheap auto shop on 82nd and Stark. We had already stopped two times to cool the engine down and after we let it cool the third time we tried to start up the engine but it wouldn't start! All of our hope vanished. Luckily, we managed to roll the car into a nearby parking lot. Since we were stuck there we decided to get a bite to eat at a small Japanese restaurant. As we waited for our food to be ready, I remembered what we had been going through the past month. Then it occurred to me that if we could get through a month of this, we could get a few more blocks. Soon my mom and I were filled with hope. We found the strength to go outside and start pushing. Sadly, we just couldn't make it. Then I asked my mom if she could try to start the car up again. She still didn't think it would work but she gave it a shot. Amazingly, it started up! In the end my mom and I drove the rest of the way and got our car fixed up.

"This I believe. Failing is not failing unless you give up all hope." If you fail a test that's unfortunate, but at least you tried. Even if you didn't study you're not a complete failure. I've got a lot of answers wrong, but who hasn't? I still would have respect for them as long as they didn't give up. I've had state writing essays and got almost all threes. But at least I didn't give up all hope. You can fall then get up and get over it and look for better days. Or, you can just sit there and feel sorry for yourself. It's all about you, you make the decisions good or bad. This I believe.

I believe that practice makes perfect. I have believed in this ever since I started playing sports in the second grade. I think that no matter what, it is you're doing. The more you work at it the better you will get. Whether it's in sports, math, video games or chugging water.

I remember how just this past year in baseball season how hard we worked to get higher in the batting order and when games started all that practice had got me fourth in the line-up. I was so proud of myself knowing that all those hours in the batting cage had paid off.

Before I found that practicing makes you much much better I spent way too much time doing things that shouldn't be important to me, like video games. Even though I was good at them it wasn't something that I wanted to be good at. Now I know that it wasn't the right choice but when I did these stupid things it made me realize what I could be doing. Everyone still has the right to chill a lot but always remember that things that matter to you, you should work on more. This I believe!

I believe in perseverance. Perseverance helps with everyone's challenges, jobs, school, and sports. It helped me in football last year. I was a tail back and I got tackled lots of times. I learned that you keep going when life hits you,. Perseverance motivates me not only in sports like football or wrestling, but in daily life too. Homework is a big hassle in my life. Perseverance keeps me going.

Perseverance not only helps me in sports, but my family and other people having problems in this bad economy. Perseverance builds character, and with good character you can get good grades, a winning team, and a disciplined life. Without perseverance you would have a lazy life and give up on everything you do. Perseverance is the number one thing that everyone should have and do.

Thoughts and feelings are all different colors. When you feel embarrassed or mad you are red. When you're sad and depressed you are blue. When you are silly or happy you are yellow. What color are dreams? Dreams are thoughts too. Dreams are a start of a future. At first I didn't know what a dream was. One day I saw a sign right next to the park I went to since I was 6. It reported to the whole neighborhood that it was getting torn down. I didn't know what to do. That was my favorite place to cry, read, think, and play. I was listening to the radio one morning and heard the dj on the radio say get your voice heard right here. That gave me an idea. So I called the radio station (with my parents permission) and told them what happened. They agreed with my idea so on May 2nd, 2008, I called the radio station again. The dj put me on the air and I spoke. I had no idea what I was saying. The next day I went to the park one last time. Even though, my voice wasn't loud enough, I tried to stick up for my rights. I was proud of myself for trying. That day, I learned to never give up but at the same time, I've learned life doesn't go in a straight line. That's why the world is round.

I believe…

Perseverance

I believe that mistakes are good. Mistakes are tools that some should learn from.

Thomas Edison failed over 1,000 times before he finally made no mistakes in building his light bulb. Without 1,000 tries, the light bulb would be a question today. Each time Edison made a mistake while building the bulb, he learned from it. "Next time if I changed this, then that will start to function properly," Edison might've stated. I believe that your first try for anything, should result in a failure because, what would a person accomplish if they knew they could not fail?

During a math test, I made quite a few mistakes resulting in not an ideal grade, a C. Because of this result, I learned that on my next test, I should be sure to study hard, and make sure I know the information that is being tested. Slowly, my grade rose back up to an A. As human beings, we all make mistakes and failures, but it's how we learn from them that separates us. There are great leaders that choose to turn their mistakes into something positive, but there are a lot of people that reflect on their mistakes, and turn them into something very negative.

Mistakes are good.

    The story I'm going to tell is sad, but it has a good message to it. When I was six years old, I burnt my leg. I was living in rural Oregon and my parents had to burn all the excess tree branches and things like that. So every two months or so we would put it all in a big pile and burn it. My dad would throw gas on the fire to get it started. So of course my brother, who is two years older than me thought it would be a good idea to start his own fire. He went to our garage and got the gas. Then he threw it in an ark. Now I was standing in the way of this and there was now a trail of gas from the fire to my leg. Now none of us noticed that until the fire had actually followed the trail of gas all the way to my leg. I got third degree burns from my knee to the top of my shoe. I was terrified but I finally got the fire put out by myself. My brother was standing there with a dumbfounded look on his face. Now after that I spent three months in the hospital and had two surgeries. After I healed from those surgeries, I had to go in for another surgery. After that I came home and had to use a walker for two months. When I finally went back to school I always had to have my leg up when sitting and I couldn't stand without someone's help. I still can't stand for more than five minutes without my leg hurting. I learned many things from that experience but here is the most important thing I learned: I believe in living your life to the fullest, because you never know when something might happen that makes it impossible to do the things you want to do.

I believe in failure, because failure reveals character. When you fail, do you cry? Or do you suck it up? Do you embrace failure? Look at all the athletes. Big names right? Do you watch their reactions or faces? You can see it in their faces when they lose a big game. They can taste the awful taste of defeat. It's bitter. But, what do athletes do when they lose? They try to get better. They hit the gym. Run and lift weights. When you fail, it's about how or what you do next. You can cry, or you can improve. Success builds character, failure reveals it. Next time you miss a free throw, drop the ball, or get a D. Take a second look at yourself. Failure reveals character. Approach everything carefully. Your not chasing perfection. Take your time and improve. You are what you say you are. Bad boys aren't always terrible, they all at times taste failure. This I believe.

I believe that you can do anything if you work hard enough.

I started playing football in the fourth grade. Scared to even touch the ball I refused to play offense. I thought that I would get yelled at if I made the wrong decision, I felt like there was too much pressure on me. But I was wrong.

For the next 3 years I watched the game of football on television. Learning moves to break tackles, catch the ball, and protect the ball.

In the summer I perfected my form to catch the ball.

Months later we were playing our third game of my seventh grade football year. Still on the sideline during offense, our team was struggling to gain yards. Finally Coach called my name.

First time in the offensive huddle and I was pretty nervous. I slowly gathered the play as it came out of our quarterback's mouth. I went to the tight end position. This play I was getting the ball.

The ball was snapped and I went to it for the hand off. Grabbing the ball every running back and receiver went through my head. Ronny Brown, Landainain Tomlinson, Reggie Bush, and Dallas Clark. All of them.

I went full speed through the hole dodging tackles and gaining yards. I broke out of traffic. Nothing but green in front of me.

You can do anything if you work hard enough.

I believe that you can do anything you set your mind to do. If you want something bad enough you will make it happen. If it takes practice to do it then practice as much as you can. If you need special equipment then find a way to have what it takes for you to get it and use it.

I know from life's experiences that when you make up your mind to do something and stick to the belief that you can do it, then there should be nothing to stop you.

I have started things in my life then let myself down by not finishing them. When this happened I was very disappointed in myself. But for all the times I was able to finish what I wanted to do it made me a stronger and happier person. It made my life more gratifying and that is what I believe.

-Staff

I believe in the power of persistence.

When I was in school I was a pretty good student. I was always top of my class in Math and did really well in Science and even Social Studies. However when it came to Language Arts and Writing, my teachers could not understand why I found it so hard.

I struggled all through school, particularly with writing and spelling. Where I grew up students had to take an English test at 16, which students had to pass to go to college. I passed all my other classes with flying colors (A's and 1 or 2 B's) but unfortunately I failed my Language Arts test. The test is only given twice every year so I took it again in the fall of my Junior year and failed again. I got exactly the same grade as the first time.

I was sad, and my parents tried to help me, but when I re-took the test again in the spring, I got exactly the same grade again. This time I was scared because I knew I would have to pass to get into college and I was starting my applications. I only had two more tries during my Senior year of high school.

I went to college interviews and was offered places at some great colleges to study engineering, but they were all provisional on me passing this test. My parents hired a tutor and I took it again in the Fall. When I failed again I wanted to stop going to school. "What was the point? I wouldn't get to go to college". Then my Math teacher could see I was starting to give up in other classes and offered to help. So with the help of a tutor and my Math teacher, I went into the test one final time – it would be my last try.

I can still remember that day waiting for my last try, but even more vivid is the day that I received my results. I did not dare open the envelope. It sat on the kitchen counter for a long time before I summoned up the courage when my parents came home. A "C" – Wow! The feeling that gave me was much better than the feeling I had when I got "A's" in my other classes.

I could go to college! The first person in my family to do so! I almost gave up but thankfully didn't because I love what I do now. I would not be where I am today if I had not been persistent.

In this I believe!

-Staff

America accept
accomplishment
core **believe** hope
concept confident
important hopeful
mind **pride** power
others priceless

PRIDE

proud streets
vital walk value
well trust

My grandmother recently told me a story of when she was in Germany as a kid. It was a terrible time, WWII. My great grandmother and her had to go into bomb shelters over nights and when they would come out they would find that parts of the roof of the house had caved in on their beds and they wouldn't be able to sleep in them.

They had friends and family die. They didn't have much money or anything for that matter. My great grandfather died fighting in the war on the German side. How much worse could it get? Well, German soldiers took his saber and uniform plus anything else war related of his. I've never heard much about him. While they didn't have much my great grandmother tried not to lose the little they had so she took care of it all.

But, they had hope that they would make it through and pride to keep that little bit. With hope and pride they got through it all until she met my step great grandfather. He met them while he was evacuating a bomb shelter as an American soldier. They fell in love, got married and he brought them back to the states. My great grandmother was so grateful and proud that she had notes on every piece of furniture in the house saying not to leave fingerprints on the furniture and she cleaned nonstop. What this story made me realize is that no matter how little you have, you need to take care of it and treat it well. Be proud and have hope because you can make it through any troubled times.

This I Believe

    Be proud to walk through the streets of America and be hopeful that others will be as well. Treat whatever you have well, no matter how little you have. You will make it through troubled times

I believe that pride is an important core concept. Throughout my life, I didn't really pay much attention to the importance of values like pride. I just lived everyday not really caring or noticing that I could improve myself by being proud of who I am and what I do. But after awhile, I began to finally understand this important core concept.

I began to understand pride during a basketball game. It was the bottom of the fourth quarter, and my team was losing by twelve points. We were trying so hard, but it wasn't getting us very far. We were still losing the game, and we began to lose faith in ourselves.

Although my whole team was disappointed, I felt as if I was doing the worst of all. Even though I was doing really well on defense, my offense could have used some improvement. And for some reason, I thought that my team was losing because of me. Yet, I still had that little voice in my head telling me that I could do it. I knew that if I tried hard enough that I could succeed and help my team win. So, I kept this in mind, and tried my hardest to achieve it.

When the buzzer went off, I looked up toward the scoreboard. The final score was 42 to 35. My team had won the game.

When we congratulated the other team, we all let out little screams of joy and celebrated our victory. Yet, with all of the happiness around me, I still felt a little disappointed. I didn't think that I did as well as I could have. It just felt a little uncomfortable and awkward being around all of the excitement, when I didn't feel like I deserved it. I tried my hardest, but for whatever reason I didn't think that was good enough.

I replayed my memory of the game in my head over and over again, and every little mistake I made seemed to stick out like a sore thumb. I couldn't shake the feeling of disappointment and failure out of my mind. I didn't know what I was going to do. But luckily, my teammates did.

Just as I was about to reach my highest point of disappointment, my teammates came up to me and told me how well I did. They said that I was excellent on defense, and that they couldn't have won the game without me. As they continued to explain their opinions on how well I played in the game, I began to re-think my own reflection on my performance. I started realizing that I was being foolish in thinking that I didn't do great. Although I didn't do the best on offense, I did really well on defense. I know that without me there wouldn't have been anyone back to stop the other team from scoring, which means my team wouldn't have won. And, I know I couldn't have done it without my team.

So as I finally began to realize this, I noticed that I did really well no mater what, because I tried my best, and that's the only thing that counts. The most important thing is to try hard, and never give up. And, I did that. I realized that I wasn't being very fair to myself. I did really well, and I need to realize that, and be proud of who I am and what I do.

So in the end, pride is an important core concept. You have to accept yourself, and be proud of who you are. You are you, and you can't change that. You live one life, so you have to live it right. You have to be proud of yourself no matter what. Pride is one of the most important values because it represents who you are. You have to be proud of yourself. This I Believe.

I believe in pride. I believe you should never be ashamed to have to try again tomorrow. This belief came to me sitting against a boulder on the top of Mt. St. Helens. This is how it happened.

About a year and a half ago, my friends in my boy scout troop and I started a trek up to the top of Mt. St. Helens. It was cold, dark and rainy, It was very dangerous for climbing, and we made little progress. After I lost my hat to a sudden gust of wind and one of my friends fell to his knees from the gale, we decided we were in over our heads. We were very close to the top, so having to turn back was heartbreaking. Still, even if we kept going to the top, we couldn't see anything. The horizontal rain was like needles on my skin. I whispered a silent message to the mountain as we turned around, "I'll be back." I swallowed my pride and we went home.

Several months later, in late August, we returned to the mighty mountain. Our group was much smaller this time around. It was a clear and sunny day, but very windy. The gusts reminded me of our previous attempt, and of the agonizing taste of defeat. I shook those thoughts out of my head. Today was a fresh start. We began our journey up the mountain. As usual, we had to take a trail through a mile or two of forest before we could access the actual mountain. When we cleared the woods, I could see the full mountain for the first time. It was beautiful and hideous at the same time. Its monumental beauty mocked its enormous size, and yet it seemed grotesquely deformed. Almost as if it had exploded and dumped its contents on one side of it (which, in essence , it had). The so-called "trail" was merely a winding line of stakes in the ground that marked where it was stable and where it was unstable. We marched up the mountain, climbing over boulders, jumping across enormous crevasses, and crawling through tunnels made by the constantly howling winds. We soon neared the weather stations, a fenced off plaza of bizarre instruments and devices, and ate lunch. This is where I realized what I believe in. Leaning against the boulder, eating lunch, staring in awe at the wonderful beauty before me.

I thought deeply about it, and realized that if I had kept going that day, if we summited in near total darkness and horizontal rain, I never would have come back. I never would have seen the wide open landscape before me. I never would've realized that it's okay to try again. A gust of wind broke my concentration. Lunch was over, and it was time to finish what we started. The last half mile or so was through what is known among the hiking community as "skree". Skree is essentially busted glass. It is sharp, chunky, sharp, abundant, sharp, painful and did I mention it's sharp? It tears at your boots and rips through the rubber on them, ruining a perfect pair of boots in minutes. With little more than a nod to my companions, I strapped on my goggles and marched up the slope.

When the time finally came for me to take the last step onto the peak of the mountain, I smiled and felt my pride rushing back to me. I knew I had done it. I had accomplished what I previously failed at. I had regained something I left on the mountain last time, and it wasn't my hat. It was my pride. That's what I believe in.

I believe in many things. Trust, hope, friendship, the power of laughter. But pride was nothing I had in mind until I graduated from the sixth grade. I learned that, not only should I work my hardest on all assignments and projects, but also to take pride and know that I did a very good job.

During my sixth grade year, I was one of the top students in my class. My classmates called me "the Nerd" or "Mr. Know-It-All". They all predicted that I got straight 6's on my report card and expected me to get 100% on all tests. I knew they were joking around, they were my friends. But sometimes, I got insecure in my abilities and believed that I was really overdoing everything.

On the very last day of school, all parents of sixth graders, the sixth grade teachers, the principals and vice principals, and the whole sixth grade student body attended a sixth grade graduation ceremony. I was so sad to be leaving elementary school, and potentially lose some friends. But I was ecstatic for the summer break coming up.

Each teacher began to hand out certificates in front of the whole crowd. The first one was the the "President's Education Awards Program". I had heard of it, but was certain that it would be an honor to receive such a certificate.

One by one, students walked up to their teacher to get their certificate. Once my teacher stepped up to the podium, he called my name. Overwhelmed, I got up in front of everyone. My friends were cheering me on. As the list went on, more and more of my friends joined me.

This made me believe in pride. Through the year, I didn't know that I would end up with such an award. I thought that each assignment I turned in would just cause people to think differently of me. But in the end, I got something that is priceless to me, a sense of accomplishment.

In the 6th grade I created a Van de Graff electrostatic generator for a class science show. When I presented my project to the class, everyone was amazed. The generator worked flawlessly and discharged as it was supposed to. I was so proud of my creation.

I had worked long and hard to finish my project for class. My dad and I toiled to finish the generator by the deadline. The Van de Graff generator was built and refined with parts from my dad's shop. When it was finished, and successfully tested, I was so proud. Anyone could have bought a generator and built one from instructions, but I had created one with rubber bands, PVC pipe, mixing bowls, and a power drill.

Showing off my brainchild to my class only made me prouder in myself. The class "ohh"d and "ahh"d at the sight of what looked like a pillar with a sphere on top. I gave my speech with confidence induced from the audience's rapturous attention. Emboldened by my speech, I started up my contraption and, literally, let the sparks fly. First, shocking a metal ball, then another student, the presentation went off without a hitch. My pride in myself and my creation only grew after the other presentations. To me, no other project garnished as much interest as my generator.

Creating a Van de Graff electrostatic generator was a very proud moment in my life. Building with parts from my dad's shop, and presenting the generator endowed me with confidence in myself and my abilities. Pride is good in moderation, and vital to being confident in yourself. This I believe.

Pride is the event I am describing. Something happened during the summer when I finished 7th grade. It was August and I just bought a boxing bag. I began losing weight and getting much stronger, but it was time to start school. As school went on, I began seeing that there are a lot of wrong things with my health. It was not December and I had lost 25 pounds, now I was weighting 138. But it still didn't seem right. Now weighting 128 I'm fitting in with everyone. What I did in the summer of 2009 is what I take pride in.

believe
Believe
accept
create
brain **best** fear
career
devoted education
different
doubt imagination hatred
individuality help
knowledge
mind leadership
miracles nature
remarkable
music power success
thoughts time
skill soul
understand wisely
world
try

I believe in skill. Skill is the one thing that everyone needs for a career. Unfortunately, for me I never had the skills to do even the simplest of things such as mowing the lawn, taking out the trash, and of course doing the dishes. I was always the kid who would try but always screwed up in a way that made me look stupid. Because of this, until this day I hesitate to do even small things for fear that I will mess up and get laughed at for it. Same thing with words. Also for fear that I';ll say something that either makes no sense or of course something dumb so that people can make fun of me. But even for someone like me who can't do simple things there is always some sort of skill that can be used somewhere. For instance I'm really good at video games. Then you ask where is that going to get me. Well it's not going to get anywhere with that here. But I heard that in Japan you can be famous just for being awesome at video games. See that's why I believe in skill because of skills that you think are useless can be used in some sort of way that can still help you make quite a bit of money. You know $$$$$.

I believe in imagination to create unbelievable things to make this a better world.

When I was in fourth grade, I encountered an event that took a lot of imagination to complete. The object was to create a house with furniture and accessories in it, with a sheet of graph paper. From the silence and darkness the classroom contained, I was able to picture it in my mind. For instance, anyone that owned a room would prefer to have a restroom near it, so that was the method I used to decide where to plot the furnitures.

Sadly, I had a budget, so I couldn't express my imagination to its max limit. Since it was a class project each student had a different budget. The budgets were determined by pulling a piece of paper out of a plastic bucket and on the papers were the budget amounts. When I think back three years ago about the assignment, I feel like I was a professional drafter. I also felt like I was creating my future mansion.

Before this event occurred I thought that this was just a regular homework assignment to get a better grasp of area and perimeter. Later on, I finally noticed that the assignment was to increase our strengths of imagination. Some values that were important to me back them were just to quickly finish my homework and play games. Now, I think education is really important along with the support my family provides.

I believe that we all should use our time wisely before it is taken away. Not so long ago, at home, I heard a quote said by my grandma when I refused to do my homework, "Use your time wisely, as you are still young." I couldn't understand the first time, but my parents and grandma explained it to me in our living room.

What they said was they couldn't do the stuff that I can do. They told me I was still young. I thought my grandma was the smartest for her age. She told me she forgo some things as she continued aging. But she is proud of doing the things in the past to make my future possible. If my grandma never met my grandpa, they wouldn't have had my mom. If my dad never met my mom, then I wouldn't have been born.

I then realized the difference between my grandma and me. I run, and she walks. I stand, and she sits. It all became clear to me. My life would be nothing if I grow older, unless I make use of it.

When I think back on this day, it makes me feel lucky to understand that I'm still young inside. Before this event, I thought that I could be able to do stuff, that I can do now, as I age. Now I know that I should use every second, minute, days and even year wisely, or I won't have the chance again. I believe that we all should use our time wisely before it is taken away.

Click, clack, click, click, clack. I hear the march, like the beat of my shoes tapping the wet pavement. I look down at my legs and see peachy, red, tired limbs. My side ache is mild, but not as bad as the first time I ran a 5K.

I believe in effort because without it, I wouldn't have made it this far in running. (No pun intended). Every week I run about three times or more. Also, I compete in cross country races. Even if I'm not the first girl to finish a race, I'd love the fact I won my own special sense of effort. Knowing you put effort into something is an awesome experience that could be described in a few words. Symptoms of effort may include happiness, pride, and exhaustion.

Sadly, I have to leave you. It's for a good cause though. I am leaving for the rest of my run. Maybe I can get home fast enough for dinner.

I believe fighting is not the answer. We should try to solve our problems with words. When I was seven I kicked my sisters two front teeth out because I was mad about something she said. Now looking back I see that was not the right thing to do. I should have talked it out because I made her teeth fall out and her face started bleeding. This did not solve any problems for me that day. So I believe that no one should ever have to fight with any other person again. I believe the world should talk about their problems. I believe fighting is not the answer. We should talk out our problems. When I kicked my sister no one gained anything because i lost control. I should have at least talked to my sister, fighting is not the answer. This I believe.

I believe that music fills our souls but our personalities are the shell that holds it inside. In each of us is a beat. That beat describes who we are. The instrument describes how we live. Great musicians didn't learn how to play, they learned how to find it. To be a musician is to be more unique than anybody else. That takes courage. You can play a song but it will be slightly different than everybody else. You cannot show somebody how to play music correctly. You have to let them express themselves. Any state, any country, we are the same but are also different.

I believe in the power of nature.

Bright and early one Saturday morning I woke, packed my bags and got in the car. During the long ride to the gorge, I rested. I was as tired as if I had already hiked the 12 miles that I was preparing to undertake. As soon as I arrived, the rest of my group pushed us to get started and I barely had time to glance at my surroundings. We continued this pace for the first 8 miles and during that time I went slower and slower until finally I had to rest. We stopped by a small creek with sparkling blue water of the most rich color. As soon as I paused to admire my surrounding I had energy and I felt better. On the way back (the last 4 miles) I took special care to notice my surroundings by the end of the hike. Nature really does have incredible power. We need to get out in nature more. This I believe.

Sometime in everyone's life they have killed an animal. That could be a fly, mouse or even a rabbit. Most people don't think about it unless they hit something with their car. And they don't care if they kill a bug, but I believe all animals deserve respect.

Just because insects are small, it doesn't mean that they don't have lives. Most people kill flies because they think they're gross. Flies may have a horrible job, but is that any reason to try and kill them? That's like trying to kill the garbage man every time you see him.

Some animals look bad but that doesn't mean you shouldn't be nice to them. If you see a stray pet you should help it. Maybe give it some food and take it to a place like the vet where the owner can find it.

I believe you should be kind to all animals. That is what I believe in.

"Dogs bring happiness" That's what everyone with a dog had told me when I was a kid. I always told them off. Saying that doge were too messy and high maintenance. I never thought about how they could bring love, or endless smiles. This all changed 10 months ago.

I was in 6th grade. It was around springtime, I remember because I was just two weeks away from going to outdoor school. As I slipped on my white Clackamas sweater, I was all smiles. Today was the day that we would pick up our new six week old puppy, a pure breed golden retriever.

I hopped in the car. I was only thirty minutes away from my new dog, Lucy. That's what we had agreed to name her. When we pulled up to the house I quickly opened the door, not waiting for the car to come to a halt. I glanced both ways before crossing the street. I was in downtown Portland, standing in front of a white house with a one car garage. In the front yard there were nine golden retriever puppies. I walked up the steps. I noticed that four of the puppies had collars. This wasn't unusual because some of the puppies had already been chosen. A man that somewhat resembled Homer Simpson and a very tan looking girl emerged from the front door. They shook hands with my dad and brought out three female puppies. We had decided earlier that we wanted a female because they are much smaller. The first puppy I looked at had a dark coat. My dad picked her up and held her in his arms. I petted her and then looked at the others. The second puppy kept running away form me, so she was out. The last puppy I looked at was by far the biggest. She, also, would not let me hold her. I sighed, looked around and made my choice. I choose the dark coated puppy that still remained in my dad's arms. She was cute as a button, and I knew that she always would be. On the road home I held Lucy the whole time. As I looked out the window and saw the reflection of my new puppy I knew that the saying was true, "Dogs bring happiness."

I believe that education is the best method for combating fear and hatred. Knowledge and understanding allow people to empathize with others' situations. I believe the cure for most of what we are scared of is to learn more about it.

A dark room is only scary until the light is turned on. Knowledge is the light that often shows us that our initial fears were unfounded. The only thing we have to fear is fear itself. Our fears often lead us to distrust and sometimes even hate, the things we do not understand. I believe in education because it helps us understand the world and other people better. Knowledge has the power to eliminate myths, half-truths, and superstitions. Knowing how things work allows us to seize control and effectively manipulate our environment.

I believe that everyone should strive to be a life long learner. Education is not limited to a school or a classroom, only the limits of our imagination. We face some daunting challenges in the future and knowledge and education are the keys to solving them.

There was this one neighbor that lived right above my apartment. Of course it wasn't just him, he had his whole family there by his side. He taught me something. He taught me how to truly live life to the utmost fullest, to not just try your best, but do your best. To believe in the power of your thoughts, for they are truly unfathomable. You can say that's somewhat become my life philosophy.

It was a chilly night. The one that had me all cuddled up within the blankets. It was the perfect contender for my ideal of a good night's sleep. I was just drifting off when BAM!! Even the ceiling shook from the sudden impact coming from above. It wasn't the first time since that has happened. In fact it happened almost every night. I wanted to get some sleep. But every time I closed my eyes, there would be something that kept me awake.

The next day (after I had finally fallen asleep) I decided to confront my neighbors. My mom and I went up to the fourth floor and knocked on their front door. A women in her middle ages answered. We told her about our situation. She began to cry. My mom and I were so astounded, we didn't know what was going on at all. It was so sudden. We asked her what was wrong, but she just let the door open all out. Inside was a normal apartment. But sitting in a wheelchair was a teenage boy. I understood everything at once.

His mom told us that he was disabled and unable to properly function, nevertheless, he tried to achieve everything that he possible could. The late night rumblings were his attempts at getting in and out of bed by himself, he genuinely tried to be independent and was gradually improving. At that moment, I felt something inside me change.

We didn't ask any further questions. We deeply apologized and returned home. Once inside, I sat in deep contemplation. I've never met a disabled person before, and I certainly never gave it too much thought – other than sympathy – to them. However, hearing the story that his mom provided us with, I had an immeasurable respect for that boy. He, who was so unfortunate as to be born with such a burden, was living his life, doing everything that was possible to make the best of it.

If he was so determined to live his life, why couldn't I? He really inspires me to this day. I don't just try my best, I DO my best. Just like Yoda said "Do or do not. There is no try." Stephen Hawking is also a very admirable person. He wasn't born with the illness he now has. It started to progress during his college years. It must have been terrible being able to know what it was to be able to move around freely, and then suddenly having to spend the rest of your life in a wheelchair. Nonetheless, his disability didn't stop him from achieving great heights. He is one of the best physicists known to man.

This proves that your thoughts are truly remarkable. If one sets their mind to something, and are fully devoted, they will get there, one step at a time. I have absolutely no doubt in the power of my brain. It is the best computer in the world.

I believe people should make the best of it and have the time of their lives. I first realized this when I was 11 years old over summer vacation. I was at summer camp. One day in the middle of the week, our cabin counselors told us we were going to the lake and everyone had to participate in what we were doing next.

When we got down to the lake the counselors told us we were going to have a mud fight. What they meant by mud fight, was we were going to throw mud at everyone. Not one of us knew what to do because none of us had ever been told to throw mud at people. We were all really excited, but became nervous. Nobody did anything.

I thought it seemed fun even though we would be sopping in mud, so I decided to start the fight. I grabbed a big handful of mud and threw it. After I threw, we all got excited and actually started the fight. I am proud of myself for trying new things. I learned by trying new things, it will be nerve wrecking and exiting. I believe we should have fun and have the time of our lives. This I believe.

It was a calm morning in the Tillamook Bay. My dad and I were on a fishing trip fishing for salmon. Two hours had past and there wasn't much happening. Our rods were still, the water was calm and most importantly, there were no fish in sight. Just before we were thinking about turning back, my fishing line took 5 hard jerks and then went straight down. Startled, I raced to the rod with my dad right behind me. I gripped the soft handle with my sweaty hands and jerked the rod up. After five minutes of pulling and reeling, I heard a loud thud and the weight on the rod vanished. The fish was gone, and so was my hard work. I turned to my dad with my head drooped down and said, "I lost the fish dad, I failed". He knelt down on one knee until our heads were level, "You have not failed son, the only way you could fail is if you choose not to try again", he responded. At that moment I realized something. I realized that failure is not the act of failing to do something, it's when you choose not to try again. I have believed and relied on this statement for two years because most of the people who do not succeed the first time start to think as if that was their one and only chance, rather than even thinking of moving forward and trying again. I believe that if everyone in the world kept trying again over and over, our success rate would be 90% better. Later that day after the fishing rip, I ended up catching two 30 pound fish all because I didn't give up. I didn't fail.

I believe in individuality, because we are all different in our own way and we need to stay the way. Every thing is different about us and we need to accept that.

"Be different."

Having a little sister that's 9 years old, I respect that she looks up to me, idolizes me, and wants to be like me. I tell her "If you want to be like me, don't be like me." This reason is everyone is different and we don't need to say, do, dress or act the same.

I believe in individuality because it makes up everyone.

Last summer instead of staying home all day, I went to work with my dad 4 or 5 days of the week (not including weekends). We didn't have as much money as everyone else in the Happy Valley area so I decided to try and get something most people didn't have. So I went to work for my dad and his customers. One of the days I worked so hard, I went to sleep at 7:00 and woke up at 12:00. I was doing typical work that most teenagers do. Gardening, cleaning and helping my dad with structure and cement. I felt very proud of myself even though I came up with a third of the price my lap top cost. When my birthday came around my family understood how much commitment I had put into those hot summer days that they came up with the other two thirds. This showed me I could do almost anything if I put my heart into it. I plan on working 3 times harder this summer and saving and buying a used mustang with all my own money. This I believe.

I believe that healthy habits create happiness.

I used to believe that I needed wealth to be happy. I didn't have it, but I coveted it. I wasn't wealthy and I wasn't happy.

My father killed himself 2 weeks before my 21st birthday. I thought about choices he had been making in the years before his death, and knew that I could go down the same self-destructive path.

I began setting small goals for myself—start exercising daily, get outside, read instead of watching TV, go to bed early. Following through with healthy habits like these made me more positive towards other people. I stopped being sarcastic and started complimenting people, smiling, and listening.

The happier I got, the more I could tell I was positively impacting people around me. I could do my job with more attention and energy. I attracted positive people into my life.

Over ten years later, I continue to consciously practice these habits. Now I have the added incentive of being a good role model for my students.

It isn't monetary wealth, but my healthy habits create happiness for me, and it spreads to the people around me.

This I believe.

-Staff

I believe that we should encourage each other to try new things. We should celebrate each others' creativity, whether it's amazing or not, because either way great things can and will grow from it.

When I was a freshman in high school, I was given the task of creating an open-ended project on Shakespeare's "Romeo and Juliet." My friend Jeremiah and I decided to make a video from little construction paper cutouts resembling South Park characters. The video was low quality, hard to understand, and looking back on it, awful. But my classmates celebrated my creativity, and gave me compliments on trying something new. My teacher saw the potential in this project and suggested I take video production the following year.

I ended up taking video production for the rest of high school, and started working at a local public access TV station at age 16. I was a TV producer and editor in college, and trained other college students to create videos, as well as creating movies myself. I then co-founded "Epicenter Media," a video production company where I made professional videos for weddings and music events. I am now a media arts teacher and teach middle school kids to make videos and pursue their creative endeavors.

I can trace the course of my life back to my 9th grade English class and the reaction my classmates had to my video project. Had they given me harsh, non-constructive criticisms, I think that the course of my life would have been totally different and wouldn't have the magic of video production in it. That is why I believe that we should be supportive and celebratory of others' creative endeavors. We should encourage each other to explore new sides to ourselves because even if it's totally dorky, great things can come from trying new things.

-Staff

Doing the dishes, doing homework, doing the Saturday morning chores - these are the bane of childhood for many kids growing up in a home like mine. As I travel the road back into those years and paths to those specific experiences, however, I have come to realize how important - actually, how wonderful - these mundane duties really are.

Growing up with parents who were both teachers meant that evening homework was as routine as brushing teeth. There was no escape ... for any of us. Though we might spread out a bit, we were "together" in our evening quest to learn and prepare. In retrospect, I have come to realize that the commonality of our daily tasks united us in significant ways. It also promoted ongoing "conversations" about what each of us was doing at school, what we thought about those experiences, and the questions that these experiences propogated. Through the "sporadic conversations," we not only became more intimately intwined in each others' worlds, we also become each others' teachers and mentors. While my education was supported, if not accelerated by these evening sessions, the most important "product" was the opportunity it afforded my parents to transfer their more significant vlaues to me - values that now guide my life and my interactions with my own children.

Like many thousands of wonderful meals my mom prepared for me as a kid, I don't remember any one specific conversation any more than I remember any one specific meal. Nevertheless, I do know that like those meals, the evening homework sessions "fed" me very well. They provided me with the critical support all kids need. They most definitely helped me learn, and they most definitely enabled me - and continue to enable me - to face life with a well-endowed set of guiding values and beliefs.

Therefore, I believe that the routine, day-to-day chores - even chores like homework - are what build us into the strong and well-prepared adults of our future.

This I believe.

-Staff

I believe in family, in laughter, in kindness and beauty. I believe in doing the right thing because it's the right thing to do.

Growing up with a strict mom that always worked hard taking care of our family of six makes me wonder at her dedication. My dad, a funny scholar, involved in the community and admired by many is known for his clever wit. I believe in the strength and love of family and the joy that laughter brings.

Having a little sister with special needs has given me a deeper appreciation for the simple acts of kindness. Hurting people, teasing kids that are different from you is just wrong. I believe in kindness. It is the right thing to do!

As an art teacher and mother I see the beauty in many things. I enjoy the beauty in my students' hearts and in their works. I love the beauty of NATURE, like admiring all the colors that make up the sky at dusk with my daughter Cassidy, or noticing the way the persimmon hold on to the tree long after the leaves have fallen and embarrassing Taylor as I stop to take a picture.

Because of family, I believe in all these good things.

-Staff